CHRONICLE ✦ OF AMERICA™

AMERICAN REVOLUTION

1700–1800

JOY MASOFF

SCHOLASTIC REFERENCE

History Advisors:
Mary Beth Norton
M. D. Alger Professor
of American History,
Cornell University

Robert Stremme
Elementary School and
College Educator

Library of Congress
Cataloging-in-Publication Data

Masoff, Joy, 1951– · American revolution,
1700–1800 / by Joy Masoff. · p. cm.—
(Chronicle of America) · Includes bibliographical
references (p.) and index. · Summary: Re-creates
the American colonies before, during, and after
the American Revolution by describing in
words and pictures various aspects of the
colonists' lives, including work, food, clothing,
shelter, religion, events leading to the war, and
life as a soldier. · 1. United States—History—
Revolution, 1775–1783—Juvenile literature. ·
2. United States—History— Revolution,
1775–1783—Pictorial works—Juvenile literature.
· 3. United States—History—Colonial period, ca.
1600–1775—Juvenile literature. 4. United States—
History—Colonial period, ca. 1600–1775—
Pictorial works—Juvenile literature.[1.United
States—History—Revolution, 1775–1783.
1.United States—History—Colonial period, ca.
1600–1775.] I. Title. II. Series. · E208.M357 ·
2000 · 99-053695 · 973.3—dc21 · CIP
ISBN 0-439-05109-6
10 9 8 7 6 5 4 3 2 1
0/0 01 02 03 04
Printed in Mexico 49
First printing, August 2000

TABLE OF CONTENTS

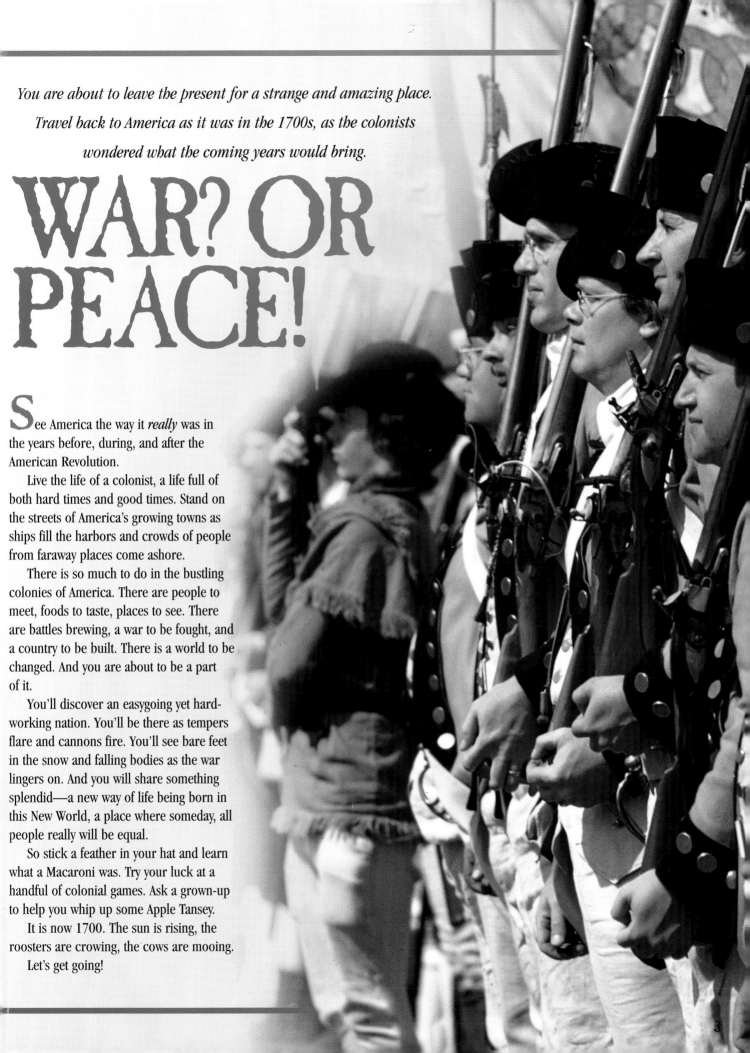

You are about to leave the present for a strange and amazing place.

Travel back to America as it was in the 1700s, as the colonists

wondered what the coming years would bring.

WAR? OR PEACE!

See America the way it *really* was in the years before, during, and after the American Revolution.

Live the life of a colonist, a life full of both hard times and good times. Stand on the streets of America's growing towns as ships fill the harbors and crowds of people from faraway places come ashore.

There is so much to do in the bustling colonies of America. There are people to meet, foods to taste, places to see. There are battles brewing, a war to be fought, and a country to be built. There is a world to be changed. And you are about to be a part of it.

You'll discover an easygoing yet hard-working nation. You'll be there as tempers flare and cannons fire. You'll see bare feet in the snow and falling bodies as the war lingers on. And you will share something splendid—a new way of life being born in this New World, a place where someday, all people really will be equal.

So stick a feather in your hat and learn what a Macaroni was. Try your luck at a handful of colonial games. Ask a grown-up to help you whip up some Apple Tansey.

It is now 1700. The sun is rising, the roosters are crowing, the cows are mooing.

Let's get going!

3

As the sun rose across America, on January 1, 1700,

it glistened on soaring mountains, sparkling lakes, and rolling meadows.

But who owned this land?

Why were so many people fighting and dying for the right to say…

THIS LAND IS MY LAND?

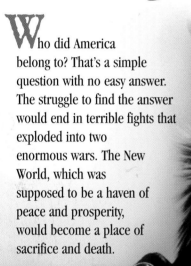

Who did America belong to? That's a simple question with no easy answer. The struggle to find the answer would end in terrible fights that exploded into two enormous wars. The New World, which was supposed to be a haven of peace and prosperity, would become a place of sacrifice and death.

THIS WAS MY LAND FIRST!
★

For 35,000 years, people had lived quietly on this vast continent. When the first Europeans stumbled onto America's shores, there were more than 300 Native American nations spread out across the land. Some nations got along well with the others. Some didn't. The Native Americans spoke hundreds of different languages and worshiped different spirits. Every group had their own special ways of doing things. Then, within the blink of an eye, the Europeans came and changed their world forever.

Diseases spread by the Europeans claimed the lives of three-quarters of the Native Americans. Less-than-honest "trades" and "deals" cost them much of their ancestral lands. As more and more people arrived from across the Atlantic, the Native Americans were slowly pushed out of their homes.

I CLAIMED THIS LAND FOR MY KING!
★

"Mine! This place is mine," the Europeans cried as they dropped their ships' anchors and planted flags on America's sandy shores. "In the name of the king…or the queen…I claim this land for *my* country."

Those European countries were the most powerful in the world. But they had one problem. They didn't have enough land. Land meant farms and food, forests of trees to build warships and trading vessels, and space for big cities. Land meant power.

GET OFF MY LAND... OR ELSE!

★

The great Spanish fort at Saint Augustine in Florida still stands proud and strong.

The new arrivals claimed the Americas for Spain...for France...for Holland...for Sweden...for England. When they couldn't get land by trading with the Native Americans, they simply took it by force. Every year, it seemed they grabbed more and more.

At first there was plenty of land to go around. America was huge—far bigger than anyone even dreamed. But soon the Europeans started running into one another or grew jealous of a particularly nice spot another country had claimed. Fighting started. Wars broke out. The New World became a bloody battlefield for the Europeans.

Everywhere the Europeans went they built forts, big stone ones and sprawling wooden ones—sometimes with slave labor provided by captive Native Americans. By the middle of the 1700s there were dozens and dozens of forts east of the Mississippi River.

MY HOME, MY TOWN, MY FAMILY

★

So that's the way it was in America as the 1700s unfolded. Everything was changing, sometimes too quickly. Promises were made, then broken, and a fight was definitely brewing. But in between the threats and the fights, people were putting down roots and building houses, starting farms, and laughing and playing with their growing families. Folks were growing rich off this lovely land, building new cities, and setting out to begin settling even deeper into the center of America. To most people, America was a land of hope and happiness. But was it a land worth dying for?

Get ready to leave Europe forever. Say farewell to your loved ones. Take a long ocean crossing on a rickety sailing ship. Land in a strange port city. Try your hand at a very different way of life. Make friends from other faraway lands. That's how America became a land of...

DANDY YANKEE DOODLES

They came from England, Scotland, and Ireland...from Germany, Holland, and France. But when their ships docked at the piers in New York or Boston, they became something new. Those seasick, dog-tired folks were now Americans!

Every month, people crowded onto sailing ships and headed across the Atlantic. They came from Europe by the thousands, because they had heard that in America a poor person could become a rich one if he or she was willing to work.

THE THREE AMERICAS
★

Depending on where those people landed, they found a slightly different America.

If they sailed into the port city of Boston, they would find that the people of New England (which included Connecticut, Rhode Island, Vermont, New Hampshire, and Massachusetts) were mostly farmers and fishers. New Englanders were serious folks—hardworking and raised with a deep streak of Puritan still in them. Toil first. Party later.

The folks who docked in the Mid-Atlantic colonies—Pennsylvania, New York, New Jersey, and Delaware—found a great mingling of cultures. There were Dutch and Swedes, Germans, French, and free Africans, all learning to live side by side, adopting bits and pieces of each other's culture.

The few who ended up sailing into Charlestown, South Carolina, found that the Southern colonies (North and South Carolina, Georgia, and Virginia) were dominated by agriculture, focused especially on tobacco and rice. Plantations were far apart and there were few cities. Folks kept to themselves. People seemed poorer —and richer—here than in the rest of the country.

FARMERS IN THE DELL
★

By the middle of the 1700s, almost 40 percent of America's men and women were independent farmers. They grew just about everything they needed to live comfortably—food to fill their tummies and fibers to make their clothing.

It was a difficult life, the hardest work imaginable. In some places, one of the very things that made America so wonderful also caused trouble for the early settlers. Tall, thick trees packed tightly together were a nightmare to chop down. In other places, hundreds of rocks had to be cleared away, stone by stone, so fields could be planted.

Farmwork was backbreaking. Chores were endless, and in some parts of the country where farms were far apart, life could be quite lonely. Still, hardly anyone went hungry. In the 1700s, that was a considerable accomplishment.

MARKET DAYS AND CITY WAYS
★

Every few weeks farmers would head into town to trade the things they'd grown or raised for things they couldn't make themselves—perhaps a pig for some pots, eggs for gunpowder, a basket of corn for a length of pretty hair ribbon for their daughters. There was usually an inn or tavern where the farmer could get a cool drink on market day. There might be a blacksmith and a general store.

In cities like Boston, New York, and Philadelphia, things were changing even more rapidly. In 1700, there were 7,000 people living in Boston. By 1720, Boston's population had grown to 12,000. By the middle of the century, over one and a half million people lived in the English colonies. America's cities were swelling! The colonists had to learn to deal with new problems that city life presented.

People were packed more closely together. It was hard to keep a flock of chickens, a cow, and a sheep or two in your backyard if your neighbor's yard was just inches away. What did you do with your garbage? Houses were so close together that if your neighbor's house caught fire (which they did all the time), yours would most likely burn as well. America *did* have some growing pains.

GOD BLESS AMERICA
★

Most people in America gathered together to pray at least once a week. In many places, if you didn't go to church, you could go to jail. But, churches were far more than places to worship. Farmers who sweated and strained all week long looked forward to the chance to simply sit down at week's end. Going to church was a bit like reading a newspaper—a chance to find out what was happening to everyone, everywhere. In small towns and big cities, there was gossip to pick up on, and a chance to be entertained by a lively preacher's sermons. And for children, it offered someone new to play with besides those same old boring brothers and sisters.

THE KING'S ENGLISH
★

Three thousand miles is a very long distance. That was how far away England and its king were. There were English governors and soldiers to keep an eye on things in America, but it took months for the king to get a message and months to get an answer back. Still, Americans lived proudly under British law. They read British newspapers and pledged allegiance to the British flag. Even if folks had come from Germany or Holland, they quickly became English citizens of the Americas.

But the colonists were getting used to thinking for themselves. By the middle of the 1700s, they didn't even sound like their English cousins anymore. There were many new accents and dialects getting mushed together. A unique new way of speaking was being born.

New Englanders, the people from the Mid-Atlantic colonies, and the Southerners all had very different ways of life. But the events of the second half of the 1700s would pull all three regions together, and two bloody wars would make them one nation.

SHARING AMERICA

The English colonies weren't the only colonies on the North American continent. England only controlled the land that clung to the Atlantic Ocean. France held the territories to the north, up in what is now Canada, and a huge chunk in the middle of the continent. Spain held Florida and controlled most of the western part of America. But since fewer people had settled in the Spanish and French colonies, those places grew more slowly. The English hold on the New World became stronger and stronger simply because more and more people were flocking to live in English territories.

Spanish   French   English

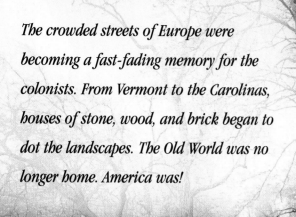

The crowded streets of Europe were becoming a fast-fading memory for the colonists. From Vermont to the Carolinas, houses of stone, wood, and brick began to dot the landscapes. The Old World was no longer home. America was!

THERE'S NO PLACE LIKE HOME

America was covered with the perfect ingredients for house building. There were forests of tall trees for lumber, and piles of stone for strong walls. The rich clay soil, when baked into bricks, was used to build homes and meeting places that could stand for centuries.

Homes in the Northern colonies often looked very different from houses in the South. Up in New England, people needed to stay warm. Down in the South, people tried to stay cool. Most northern houses had low ceilings and small windows to hold in heat, with rooms built around a big central fireplace. Farther south, where summers were hot and humid, ceilings were higher, to let heat rise away. While fireplaces were needed for cooking and warmth in the cooler winter months in the South, chimneys were always on the outside of the house. Big windows let in cooling breezes.

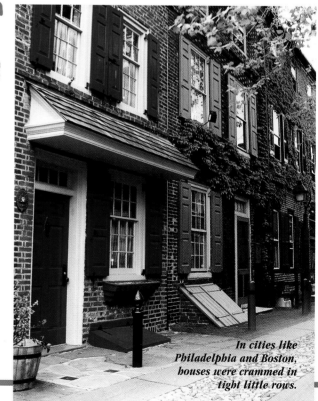

In cities like Philadelphia and Boston, houses were crammed in tight little rows.

Bedrooms weren't just for sleeping. People often entertained guests next to their beds.

George Washington lived here. This was his lovely home in Mount Vernon, Virginia.

ROOM TO GROW
★

A hall that's not a hall? A closet that's not a closet? Colonial houses were very different from ours! In the early days of the 1700s, most houses were simply one big room. That room was called the hall and it was the place where everyone ate, worked, and slept.

As families grew bigger, houses got bigger, too. Extra rooms were attached. A separate kitchen was often one of the first rooms to be added. Another add-on was the parlor, which got its name from the French word *parler* meaning "to talk"—since it was the place where people went to sit and chat. Closets were small, private rooms, a bit like a study. It was a very special honor to meet in someone's closet. There were no modern-day closets. People kept their clothes in cupboards, trunks, or chests.

Paint was very expensive, a true sign of wealth. Colonists loved bright colors, both inside and out—shockingly wild yellows, bright reds and blues—colors much more vivid than those we use today.

FROM SPRINGHOUSE TO OUTHOUSE
★

Many people had a few little buildings on the same property as their house. They might have a springhouse, which was a bit like a refrigerator—a cool place to keep food from spoiling. There was often a stable and a scullery, which was like today's laundry room. Sometimes there was a coach house, the equivalent of our garage. But the most important outbuilding was an outhouse. The colonists called them privies or necessaries—probably because it was necessary to have *someplace* to go when you had to *go*. These were located quite a distance from the main house. During the night or if the weather was awful, people used chamber pots—ceramic bowls stowed under their beds—which they emptied in the morning.

But no matter if it was a farmhouse or a manor house, to the colonists, every house was a "Home, Sweet Home."

BRICKMAKING MADE EASY

It's hard to believe that something as strong as a brick began as something soft and slimy—mud!

First, clay soil was mixed with water to make a stiff mud. The mixing was done with the feet. Then that mud was packed into wooden molds that had been dusted with sand to keep the mud from sticking. After the mud had dried a bit, the clay lump was popped out and left to sit in the sun until it dried even more. It was a disaster for a brickmaker if it rained during this step.

When the mud was hard, it was placed into a special oven and baked for 24 hours. Then, the bricks had to be cooled for two weeks. Brick-makers made a lot of bricks at each session—usually about 20,000 bricks. Lots ended up being thrown away because they had cracks and chips.

Making mud pies with his feet? Not at all! This fellow is mixing clay to the perfect consistency before pouring it into brick molds.

Shave your head, then stick a hunk of yak's hair on top. Or lace yourself up in stiff whale bones until you can't possibly breathe. You might even rub poison on your face and bugs on your lips. Here's the scoop on getting dressed in the colonies.

FROM HEAD TO TOE

Back in the 1700s, you could tell in an instant whether a person was rich or poor, from the North or the South, a backwoods farmer who had to make clothes from scratch, or a well-to-do shopkeeper.

WHAT SHOULD I WEAR TODAY?
★

Probably not underpants! Men pulled their pants on right over their bare skin. Everyone—men, women and children— wore shifts, which were long shirts that they slept in. Then they layered clothing over the shifts during the day. Men wore knee-length pants called breeches, a waistcoat (what we call a vest today), and coat. Women's clothing was a bit more complicated. Before they could pull on a dress, they had to deal with something else.

Tiny waists were the style for women, so most wore tight corsets called stays. These laced up so tightly, a woman could barely breathe. They were made of metal or bone and girls began wearing them early—sometimes as young as 18 months.

Another way to make the waist look small was to make the hips look big—the bigger the better. So, wire cagelike structures, called *panniers*, were strapped onto a woman's hips. Some stretched out to two feet wide on each side. Getting through a doorway was tricky. Sitting down was impossible!

Things were different for poor women. If they laced their stays too tightly, they couldn't work! Big panniers would get in their way doing chores, so they rarely wore them.

This young woman is being laced into her stays—a job that took at least two people. One pulled and the other held on tight.

DRESSING UP
★

After women had struggled into their stays and panniers, they could finally pull on a petticoat, or two, or three! They wore one of two styles of skirt—one that was slit open in the front to show off those petticoats, or one that was closed and revealed a ruffle around the bottom. Wealthy women chose lavish silks and satins imported from Europe and France. Less-well-off ladies wore homespun—rough cloth they wove themselves.

Every woman, wealthy or not, wore a mob cap—a circle of cotton atop her hair. There were several different sizes, ranging from teeny to huge.

GETTING WIGGY

The oddest fashion craze in the 1700s was the wig. Many men shaved off all their hair, then went out and bought someone else's.

Rich fellows had wigs made of human hair. Not so wealthy? There were wigs made from yak or goat hair. Poor? Horsehair for you! Really poor? A wig made of thread. Wigs fit tightly. The most embarrassing thing that could happen to a man was "flipping his wig." The best thing that could happen was to be a "big-wig!" Both expressions became popular during America's wig-wearing years.

Some men decided that buying someone else's hair was silly. They simply grew their hair long and tied it back.

Once a week, the wig was sent out to the barber or wigmaker to be spruced up. There, it would be cleaned, combed, and recurled. Still, many a wig was infested with lice or fleas. Very itchy!

HAIR MOUNTAIN
★

Upper-class women liked towering mounds of hair. Some hairdos reached three feet in height! On important occasions, men and women coated their hair or wigs with animal fat mixed with cinnamon and cloves. Then the whole thing was dusted with flour to make it turn white. Everyone wanted to have white or gray hair. That was a sign of age and wisdom. At fancy-dress balls, it often looked as if it was snowing inside because the powder blew off everyone's hair as they danced. For just that reason, there was a special room where you could go to redust your hair. To this day, people still say that they're going to the "powder" room to freshen up.

POISON-AND-BUG MAKEUP
★

Wealthy women wore lots of makeup to parties. Very pale skin was "in." Faces were coated with powder made from white lead (a deadly poison) and flour that had been mixed with grease. Bright spots of rouge, which means "red" in French, were dotted on each cheek and rubbed on the lips. The rouge was made from insects—crushed cochineal bugs, which were also used to dye the red coats of the British soldiers. And since many people had lost a lot of teeth to decay, they popped cork balls called *plumpers* into their cheeks to keep their faces from looking caved-in and old.

Well-to-do women wore masks when they went out in the sun. After all, people who worked in the fields had suntans, not rich women.

FANCY AND PLAIN
★

Colonial times began as colorful times for men. Gentlemen wore reds, yellows, and bright blues. They loved fancy fabrics— shiny satins, rich velvets, and yards of lace. But as war drew near, the men gave up their bright colors and chose drabber shades—browns, olives, and grays. Hats were three-cornered unless you were a farmer. Farmers wanted hats that would keep the sun out of their eyes, so they usually wore uncocked hats—hats with the brims left down.

While rich folks fussed with powdered wigs and skirts so wide they couldn't sit down, simpler folks had to make do with much less. Some even had to make their clothes from scratch, beginning with a wooly sheep, or a kind of plant, called flax. Average people had only two or three sets of clothes. They wore the same thing almost every day. But that created a problem—a smelly problem. Most people only took baths a few times a year and there was no deodorant in the 1700s. Those colonial clothes reeked!

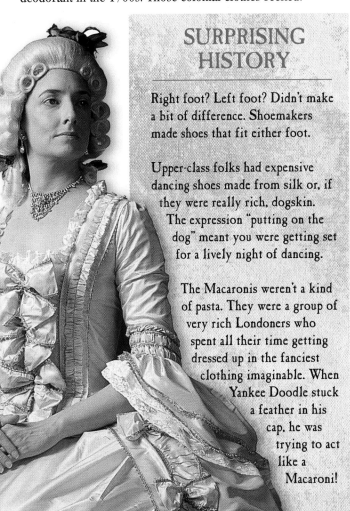

SURPRISING HISTORY

Right foot? Left foot? Didn't make a bit of difference. Shoemakers made shoes that fit either foot.

Upper-class folks had expensive dancing shoes made from silk or, if they were really rich, dogskin. The expression "putting on the dog" meant you were getting set for a lively night of dancing.

The Macaronis weren't a kind of pasta. They were a group of very rich Londoners who spent all their time getting dressed up in the fanciest clothing imaginable. When Yankee Doodle stuck a feather in his cap, he was trying to act like a Macaroni!

Do you like fast food? In colonial times, even the fastest food took hours to prepare. A typical dinner got its start before dawn as Mother built a fire, hauled in water, picked ingredients from her kitchen garden, milked a cow or two, gathered eggs from the chickens, and hung a few dead fowl to dry.

No wonder she was exhausted when her family asked…

WHAT'S FOR DINNER?

EAT LIKE A COLONIAL AMERICAN

Why not try a real colonial recipe? Here's one for a favorite called Apple Tansey—a sort of apple omelet. You'll need:

4 apples
1 pat of butter
4 eggs beaten with
6 tablespoons of heavy cream
1 teaspoon of sugar
1 pinch of nutmeg

Get a grown-up to help you. Cut the apples into thin slices. Melt the butter in a small skillet, add the apple slices, and cook over low heat, until they are soft.

Mix the rest of the ingredients in a small bowl and pour them over the apples. Cook about 2 to 3 minutes, or until the mixture sets.

Spoon the cooked mixture into individual soup bowls and top with sprinkled sugar. Eat and enjoy!

By the time the 1700s rolled around, Americans were eating pretty well. They certainly ate better than their cousins back in Europe. Appetites were hearty, and folks chowed down on big meals—heaping platters of food that included some things that would probably make you gag.

TOO HOT TO HANDLE
★

Most meals were prepared in large fireplaces, where roaring blazes were kept burning even on the hottest summer day. Three-legged iron stands, and hooks, called trammels, supported heavy cooking kettles that weighed up to forty pounds. Sadly, quite a few of America's colonial women were injured, and even killed, in cooking accidents, since long skirts easily caught on fire and caused deadly burns. Cooking was so dangerous that many women took off their skirts when preparing meals, just to play it safe.

There were no hamburgers in plastic wrap waiting to be picked off a supermarket shelf. Animals had to be killed and butchered. When the meat was ready for cooking, the most common cooking methods were boiling, broiling, and simmering in stews.

What went into the stew pot? Anything from pigeons, ducks, and geese to deer, bears, rabbits, wild pigs, raccoons, muskrats, opossums, and beavers. Broiled beaver tail was considered a real treat. There were no refrigerators, so meats, fish, vegetables, and fruit were eaten fresh or preserved—smoked, salted, or dried in the sun.

HUNGRY ENOUGH TO EAT A...

★

Just about every meal featured meat as an ingredient. Mutton, which comes from sheep, was as popular as hamburgers are today. Pork was another favorite, especially in the South, where one man preserved his recipe for smoked ham on the inside cover of his family Bible.

How much did the colonists like meat? The recipe for Battalia Pie called for four small chickens, four pigeons, a few chopped-up rabbits, four sheep tongues, and thirty cockscombs—that red fleshy growth on the head of a rooster. Imagine digging into that!

Vegetables were mostly unloved and uneaten, although the colonists did eat peas and beans. Vegetables were cooked until mushy and gray, with hardly any nutrients left by the time they were served. No matter—eating veggies would have left no room for dessert, which the colonists adored.

SWEET TEETH

★

The colonists loved sugary, rich desserts. Sweets were gobbled up at most meals—pies, cobblers, and rich fruitcakes. And if there was no time to make an apple pie, folks made Apple Tansey—apple slices fried in butter, then covered with a sauce made of beaten eggs, cream, nutmeg, and sugar. Some ingredients were different back then, though. Eggs were much smaller.

In 1774, a new treat arrived on the American dessert scene. It was called ice cream, and the colonists went wild over it!

The colonists washed down all those desserts with a new beverage—tea. Americans took a swift liking to this hot drink, especially with a heaping helping of honey or sugar. That love of tea would play a big part in the events of the years to come, as America edged closer and closer to war.

SURPRISING HISTORY

French fries with ketchup—an American classic, right? Not in the 1700s. Colonists hated tomatoes! They were convinced they were poisonous. The colonists detested potatoes almost as much.

Americans loved hanging out at taverns and inns. Second only to church, they were a popular gathering spot. In fact many people had their mail delivered to their favorite inn!

Forks were new to America's tables in the 1700s. They had just two prongs at first, then grew to three, and finally four by the century's end. Many people carried their forks with them if they were invited to dine in someone else's home, since most hostesses had only enough for their families.

How many brothers and sisters do you have?

How'd you like to have a dozen? That's how many Paul Revere had.

How about 17? That's how many Ben Franklin had.

Try getting a minute alone with your parents with that many children!

COLONIAL KIDS

The bigger the family, the better, back in colonial times. Everyone wanted to have scads of children—to help with the housework, plant and harvest the crops, and take care of the cows, pigs, and the other children in the family. Ten kids. Fifteen kids. Even twenty kids in a family was not uncommon back then.

SUGAR AND SPICE
★

Little boys and girls were treated exactly the same when they were very young. They both wore dresses! Those dresses had strings on the back—perfect for grabbing on to when little ones tried to run away. But at the age of six all that changed. Boys were ready to become men. The occasion was marked by an event called breeching, because boys traded their skirts in for breeches. In wealthy families, boys' little heads were shaved and tiny wigs were purchased. Small-sized yet manly clothes were made. You could now tell the boys from the girls.

TOUGH TEACHERS
★

Ever bring your teacher an apple? In the 1700s, children brought in firewood. Any child who forgot would have to sit in the spot farthest from the fireplace. School was a miserable place. Students sat on hard, splintery benches. If you were bad, teachers punished, and punished hard.

They might strap a whispering stick into your mouth so you couldn't talk or clip your nose shut with clothespinlike pinchers. They hung signs around students' necks that said "crybaby" or "lazy," and they made kids wear hats that said "dunce." Imagine walking through your school wearing a hat that said "stupid!"

K-A-T SPELLS CAT
★

There were very few books. Kids learned from hornbooks—paddles with paper nailed to them, then covered with a thin shaving of cow's horn to protect the paper. Printed on the paper were the alphabet and a prayer. Penmanship was one of the most important subjects taught. Teachers didn't care if you could spell because there was no standard spelling. They only cared that your handwriting looked good.

Of course, a lot of kids never even had the chance to go to school. Outside of New England, schools were rare. The Quakers in Pennsylvania had some schools, but they were few and far between. In the Southern colonies, only wealthy kids were educated. They learned from a tutor, a person who came and taught them in their homes.

A GIRL'S LIFE...
★

Most girls didn't go to school. A few lucky New England girls went to a type of school called Dame School, where an older woman taught reading and writing. More often, girls were taught at home. After all, there was work to be done. Girls learned to read by embroidering samplers. This helped them practice their letters and numbers. They learned to add by cooking and to write by keeping a receipt book—a scrapbook that held not only recipes for yummy dishes, but medical potions, stain removers, flower dyes, and housekeeping hints.

Who had time for school when there were vegetables to be picked and cows to be milked and fed? Someone had to knead the bread dough, and turn the chicken grilling on the spit. Someone had to help mom make the soap, dip the candles, wash the clothes and iron them. That someone was a colonial girl.

AND A BOY'S
★

For most boys, having a job was far more important than book learning. Many lower- and middle-class kids were apprenticed out—sent to work for blacksmiths or carpenters to be taught a trade. Sometime between his 12th and 16th birthday, a boy was sent to live with a master craftsman. That boy was then "bound" to his master until his 21st birthday. The boy had to open the shop, clean it, gather wood and water, start a fire, run errands, and watch and learn how things were done. For the next two to four years he learned the basics of his profession, then, finally, worked at his job until his apprenticeship ended. To "graduate" he had to produce a proof-piece—something to show he knew his trade. It might be a carved chair if he wanted to be a furnituremaker, or a perfectly fitted barrel if he wanted to be a cooper. If his sample was good, he could now be called a journeyman. His apprentice days were over. He was now a grown-up.

RECESS, 18th CENTURY STYLE
★

Was colonial life all hard work? Of course not! Kids always managed to find time to play. Stilts were hard to master, but great fun once you got the hang of them. So were hoops. Boys liked to run and push their hoops with sticks. Girls tossed and caught their hoops with two sticks in a game called Graces. Bilbos—devilish little sticks with a cup on one end, and a ball attached with a string on the other—were a great way to pass the time. Quoits (a bit like horseshoes but played with small rope circles) was another favorite, as was ninepin, which is a bit like today's bowling.

Backgammon, a board game, was the 18th century's Nintendo. There were a half-dozen different ways to play. Kids also played dice games, marble games, card games, and checkers, which were called "draughts." Ice-skating in the winter and fishing in the summer were always fun. Girls had dolls to dress up and love.

But talk of war brewed in the 1770s. Soon, many youngsters found their playtime was a fond memory.

TRY YOUR HAND AT NINE MAN MORRIS

Here's a game colonial kids played in the dirt with a couple of rocks and acorns. You, of course, can play it on paper. All you need is a friend, nine pennies, nine nickels, and a drawing that looks like this. Choose either pennies or nickels for yourself, and begin by taking turns placing one coin on one of the dots. The goal? To line up three of your pieces in a row while blocking your opponent from doing the same. Capture one of your opponent's pieces whenever you complete a line of three. When one player is down to two pieces, the other player wins!

Stand up straight. Keep your elbows off the table. Don't point in public.

A few basic instructions pretty much sum up good manners nowadays.

But in colonial times, there were all sorts of rules to be followed.

MIND YOUR MANNERS

Going to a dance sounds like fun. But in the colonies, dancing was serious business. A dance was where you went to find a husband or wife, gossip about the neighbors, seal important business deals—and, oh, of course, dance.

DANCE PARTY
★

In the Southern colonies, dances were tests of endurance. There, a ball might last for the better part of three or four days. Dances were excellent occasions to pick a husband or wife. Up close, in each other's arms, you could tell a lot about a person. Did they smell bad? Did they get all huffy and puffy as they danced? Were their teeth rotting? Were they clumsy? No one wanted to spend the rest of their lives with a smelly, bad-breathed, two-left-feet kind of person.

There were very specific rules to follow. Guests didn't rush out onto the dance floor the minute the music started. The person with the highest social standing—perhaps the governor, or a wealthy plantation owner, would begin by dancing first, followed by people of lesser social standing. Folks started dancing slowly, perhaps a minuet—a gentle, easy, come-together, pull-apart dance. But as the night wore on, the speed picked up. They danced jigs and reels, line dances, and country dances—which inspired the square dances we do today.

To be able to dance well was of the utmost importance in upper-class life. Young men studied math, Greek, Latin, penmanship—and dancing.

DID YOU HEAR ABOUT...?
★

Add gabbing and gossiping to all that dancing as favorite ways to pass some time. There were no TV shows or movies in those days, no fan magazines to keep you up-to-date on the latest goings-on. So when people got together, they talked. They talked at quilting bees and corn huskings. They chatted at barn raisings and after church. Gossiping was an all-American pastime.

SNIFF, SNUFF, PUFF
★

A proper gentleman always had something special with him—an enormous handkerchief. It wasn't because he might have a cold. That hanky came in handy when the fellow stuffed a pinch of snuff in his nose. Snuff was strange stuff—a powder made of finely ground tobacco. It made a person sneeze violently, but using it was considered the height of "cool."

Everyone did it—from grandmothers to governors. Both men and women smoked, too. Colonists filled clay pipes with tobacco and puffed away throughout the day. Of course, back then, no one knew that snuff and tobacco could cause horrible cancers. So they sniffed, and sneezed, and puffed away, unaware of the harm they were doing themselves.

DO, RE, MI
★

Music was another favorite way to pass the time in the 1700s. Thomas Jefferson practiced his violin for three hours a day. Ben Franklin could play several instruments well. But there were rules to be followed even where music was concerned.

If you were invited to someone's house for dinner, you were often expected to sit and listen to the women of the family sing. You were not allowed to talk while they were singing, no matter how long they sang or how awful they sounded. Guests simply sat there, looking interested.

Women never played wind instruments—things like flutes or horns. They thought doing so made their faces look ugly, so ladies only played keyboard instruments.

FOR RICHER OR POORER
★

By the middle of the 1700s, some people in America had grown rich. Rich people were referred to as "gentle" folk, drove around in grand carriages, and lived in huge mansions. Most, however, were the "middling sort." Others were dirt-poor and called "simple" folk.

People were expected to know their place in society. Simple folk never looked gentle folk in the eye. The difference between rich and poor was vast. But in America, with hard work, and a skill, a middling person *could* become a "gentle" person. Being born poor did not sentence you to a life with no hope of ever doing better, as it did in most of Europe. And *that* made America special.

FAN TALK

No one would think of going to a ball without a fan—not even a man. Not only did a fan help cool you off when things got too hot, you could also "talk" with one. Why not try this secret language?

Take a piece of paper and fold it into a fan. Tape it at the bottom. Now, start chatting:
Angry? Hit the palm of your hand with a closed fan a few times.
Jealous? Flutter the open fan in front of your face.
Concerned? Fan really fast.
Flirty? Fan very slowly.
Not in the mood to talk? Place the tip of the closed fan against your lips.

Have you ever been punished? Perhaps you were sent to your room, or told that there would be no TV for a week. Consider yourself lucky! In colonial times, punishments were cruel. Breaking the law usually ended in pain and humiliation—even for a minor crime.

NAUGHTY, NAUGHTY!

In colonial America, justice was swift and punishments could be very harsh. A thief could be put to death for stealing a cow or a horse. When you committed a crime, you were truly "marked for life."

OUCH!

★

The most common punishment for a small crime was time spent in the stocks, two boards with holes for the ankles and a seat made from a sharpened wood plank; or the pillory, two boards with holes for the hands and head, set on posts. Folks would come and hurl rotten fruit and eggs at the helpless prisoner. Ants, wasps, and other insects, drawn by the mess on the person's face, would soon swarm around, stinging every square inch of skin. Since the prisoner's hands were held tight, there was no swatting the bugs away. Some unlucky prisoners even had their ears nailed to the planks, if they were caught lying in court.

Things could, however, get worse.

BURNED AT THE HAND

★

People found guilty of serious crimes were sentenced to be hanged. If they were lucky, and proved that they knew how to read, they might get a stay of execution, since there was a chance they would read the Bible and learn from their sins. But they would also be marked for life.

The inside top of the right thumb was branded with a hot iron. The letter *T*, for thief, or *M,* for murderer, was burned into the skin. If they were caught a second time, it was off to the gallows for them. To this day, when you are in a court of law, you will be asked to raise your right hand and swear to tell the truth. This goes back to colonial times, when court officials would check a person's right hand to see if they had ever been convicted of a crime, and branded.

JUSTICE FOR ALL?

★

If you were a white male in colonial America and found yourself in a court of law, you could be assured of a pretty fair trial. But if you were a Native American or an African, you were out of luck. You could not serve on a jury and it was rare to be called as a witness against a white man.

Married women couldn't own property and had fewer rights than unmarried women. They could not do anything without their husband's permission. But they could get punished just as severely as a man if they were found guilty of a crime.

CROWDS AT THE COURTHOUSE

★

When court was in session, it was like the carnival had come to town. Street vendors sold everything from bread to live chickens. Gamblers played cards and dice, hucksters hawked worthless potions, deals were made, and debts were settled.

Execution days were the most festive of all—a day for picnicking and partying. Hundreds would assemble to watch the hanging. The doomed prisoner would be brought in on a cart, sitting on his own coffin. Crowds would cheer, then grow silent as the prisoner was seated on a horse, the noose tightened around his neck, and the horse pushed away.

People thought twice about committing a crime after seeing that!

PIRATES AND RAPSCALLIONS

Just about the naughtiest men, and some women, too, were the pirates that roamed the seas. You may think that pirates only hung out in the Caribbean, but they were at home in any hidden cove where they could lie in wait for trading ships. The Carolinas and Virginia were crawling with pirates! One of the most famous pirates of all was named Blackbeard. (His real name was Edward Teach.) Carrying six pistols in his sash, his great beard smoking with slow-burning matches he deliberately stuck in it, Blackbeard terrified all who met him. He came to his end off the coast of Virginia when he was beheaded by a very angry British sailor whose ship he'd tried to raid.

When caught, pirates were treated quite harshly. Hanging them wasn't enough. After the hanging, the body was taken down and left in chains, to rot in the sun. That's called gibbeting, and fear of it kept many a person from choosing a pirate's life.

Jail—Colonial style! A bucket for the bathroom and a lump of hay for a bed. Chains kept prisoners fastened to the wall.

Look around you. What do you see? Things! You probably see books and shoes,

lamps and chairs, plates and rugs. The colonists needed things, too.

For those people who made what the colonists needed,

America sometimes seemed like a land of ...

ALL WORK AND NO PLAY

The bigger the colonies grew, the more goods they needed. Suddenly there were over one and a half million people clamoring for flour for bread and chairs to sit on. They needed wheels for their carriages, shoes for their feet, nails to build houses, and barrels to ship tobacco in. Who was going to make all of these things?

A TRIO OF TRADES
★

No settlement could manage without three important tradespeople. The first was a blacksmith—maker of tools and repairer of broken metal items. The second was a shoemaker. Lots of people only had *shanks-mares*, a clever way to say that their legs were their "horse." Folks walked huge distances in the 1700s—up to 10 or 15 miles a day. Sturdy shoes were a must!

The third tradesperson everyone needed was a cooper. Coopers fitted strips of wood together, then banded them with iron to make barrels. They made everything from small containers for food and drink to huge casks, used for shipping tobacco and grain to Europe.

SMITHS OF ALL SORTS
★

Blacksmiths weren't the only smiths in town. Silversmiths took hunks of fine metals such as silver, pewter, and nickel (which was called German silver), and melted, molded, hammered, and pounded them into spoons, bowls, and pitchers. Paul Revere was one of America's most famous silversmiths.

Gunsmiths were really necessary tradespeople, too, since the colonists depended on their weapons for hunting and for protection. Gunsmiths cast metal for the fittings of muskets and pistols, made gun barrels from iron, and made molds for bullets. They knew how to work with silver, brass, ivory, and bone, for those folks who wanted fancy weapons.

Whitesmiths worked with cheap metals like tin, making candleholders and other household items. And, last but not least, locksmiths made keys and bolts. People now had possessions to keep protected under lock and key!

SURPRISING HISTORY

One thing blacksmiths never did in later colonial times was make horseshoes! That job belonged to the farrier.

DOWN BY THE OLD MILL STREAM
★

Among the first things most towns built was a sawmill. Using the power of a fast-flowing stream, one sawyer could turn tree trunks into building lumber in a fraction of the time it took two people using handsaws.

Another "mill" person was the miller—someone who ground grains such as oat, corn, and rye into flour. In parts of the country where streams and rivers flowed downhill, millers used the water's power to turn a grindstone. In areas without water, they used windmills to do the same thing. The tricky part of a miller's job was to make sure the grindstones were set perfectly. Too close, and the grain would be ruined.

UPPERCASE, lowercase
★

The colonists loved to read. Newspapers and books were big sellers—ways to find out what was happening elsewhere, since travel was difficult in those days. Printers and bookbinders worked long hours, printing each and every word by filling special holders, one letter at a time. The capital letters were kept in a case on the top shelf. Noncapital letters were kept on a lower shelf. That's why we still talk about upper- and lowercase letters.

During the American Revolution, six of the forty newspapers in the colonies were published by women. Mary Goddard, who ran the *Baltimore Journal*, rarely missed a publishing deadline, in spite of severe paper and ink shortages.

TOOTH TROUBLES
★

There were no dentists in colonial times. But there were drugstores. They were called apothecaries and the fellow who worked there sold chalk for upset stomachs, and bark from the cinchona tree for fever, along with other healing herbal potions. The apothecary also pulled rotten colonial teeth, full of cavities from too many sweets.

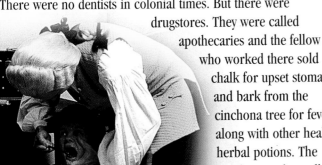

FROM SHEEP TO SHAWL
★

Textile making was a long and involved process. It took lots of people to make a simple piece of woolen cloth.

First, the sheep had to be sheared, which required strong, steady hands and *very* sharp shears. Then came the nasty job of picking through the sheared wool to pull out dried sheep dung and dirt. The cleaned wool was sometimes washed to remove the lanolin—the natural oil found in wool.

Before the wool was spun it had to be carded—the fibers all carefully lined up. Next, the spinners went to work. Wool had to be spun on a big wheel called a walking wheel. Women spun in the evening by the fire, since they didn't need much light to do it. The spun thread was wound onto a reel which flipped up when a certain length was reached. The reel was called a weasel, and the pop it made inspired the children's nursery rhyme!

After the wool was spun into thread, it was usually dyed. Flowers, insects, and roots were used to create colorful dyes, and a mordant, which is something to make color stick to yarn, was needed. Sometimes, the colonists used their own old, stale urine!

Finally, it was was time to begin weaving. A big loom was needed to do this, so most weavers were professionals. People brought their yarn in to be woven. A good weaver could produce about six yards of cloth a day.

Busy hands…long days…hard work…an opportunity to learn new skills and build a business. That was becoming the American way to work.

Have you ever done something even though, deep in your heart, you knew that it was wrong? Did you try to convince yourself it was okay because everyone else was doing it too? The issue of slavery made many Americans feel like that in the 1700s. As the colonists cried out for liberty, some people began to ask why there wasn't…

LIBERTY FOR ALL?

The land of the free? Not really! In some parts of America, half the population was slaves—people with no hope of independence, no hope for a better future.

AFRICANS FOR SALE
★

Slavery has been around since humans have, but in the 1700s a new chapter in the long, nasty history of slavery was written. The British became the largest slave traders on earth—buying and selling people who had been captured or kidnapped by evil leaders anxious to get rich *and* get rid of their rivals. In America, where a large labor force was desperately needed, how convenient it seemed to have these slaves who would work for free!

The captives came out of Africa, chained two by two, the left leg of one to the right leg of the other. They came from 1,000 different villages, speaking hundreds of different languages. They were farmers and warriors, adventurers and artists. They had little in common except for the color of their skin, a birthplace—Africa—and the fact that they were prisoners on a ship bound for a faraway land.

"PACKED LIKE BOOKS ON SHELVES"
★

That's how one person described the trip over on the slave ships. It was a horrifying experience, with people jammed into tiny compartments, some no more than 18 inches high. Eleven million Africans were dragged from their villages, and shipped overseas during the 1700s. Many died. Others jumped overboard and drowned rather than live a life in chains. Still, others somehow clung to hope, dreaming of the day when they could escape and go back to their homelands.

A LIFE ENSLAVED
★

Most of the slaves who came to North America were sold to plantation owners in the Southern colonies who grew tobacco and rice. Getting the crops harvested took many hands. It was brutal, back-breaking work.

If you were a field slave, your day began before sunrise, even though it was still dark outside. Men and women worked equally hard. Both cut down trees, dug ditches, and tended crops, bent over in the hot sun or the freezing rain. As they worked, many were constantly watched by overseers on horseback, who were often armed with whips and fierce dogs. Only when night fell could the exhausted Africans return to their cramped, small huts.

Fifteen to twenty slaves squeezed into each of these little log cabins at Carter's Grove, Virginia.

FROM "CAN" TO "CAN'T"

★

That was how slaves told time. From first light (can see) to darkness (can't see), slaves worked without stopping, resting only on Sunday. Their days were dull and boring. One man described his workplace as a field "that stretched from one end of the earth to the other." Why did they do it? Why didn't they run away?

Well, many did. Some runaway slaves hid in Florida, which still belonged to Spain. Some joined Native American groups. Others even made the very long journey to Canada, or Mexico. Still others tried passive resistance—working *really* slowly, pretending to be sick, breaking tools when no one was looking. The slave owners complained they were slow and lazy, but, in fact, the Africans were fighting back the only way they could.

TWO WHO DARED TO DREAM

There were dark-skinned men and women who managed to find fame and freedom, even in a country where they were not treated fairly.

Benjamin Bannecker was the son of free parents, and grew up on a farm in Maryland. When he was twenty-three, he decided to build a clock—the first built entirely in America—even though he had never seen one. He figured out exactly how the mechanism worked, and his clock kept perfect time for the rest of his life! But he did so much more.

Wrapped in a blanket, gazing up at the stars, Bannecker taught himself astronomy. By day, he studied mathematics and science, and for many years, he published an almanac. He also fought tirelessly to end slavery. This quiet man became known as the "Sable Genius"—a true American hero.

Twenty-year-old Phillis Wheatley, a slave in Boston, Massachusetts, had a gift—a gift for writing beautiful poetry. Her poems were collected, published, and became hugely popular. She even corresponded with George Washington, who was a great fan of her writing.

MAKING A HOME

★

As the years passed, the Africans made the best of a bad situation. Women tried to make a home life in their cramped slave quarters. In some colonies, especially in the Middle Atlantic region, slaves learned skills such as carpentry and blacksmithing. In time, slaves in the Northern colonies were freed, and many settled into life as farmers and sailors.

But in most places in America, life for people with dark skin grew crueler and crueler. They were treated as property, like a house or a horse—something that could be bought, and sold, and tossed away. Because it was difficult to tell a free African from an escaped slave, many colonists assumed that any unfamiliar dark-skinned person was a runaway slave. There was a black America and a white one. It would take centuries to right this very sad wrong.

A break from work was always welcomed. Slaves in New York celebrated Pinkster, a Dutch springtime holiday. They gave the occasion a lovely African twist, dancing and singing late into the night.

If someone asked you to give them a piece of the sky, could you? If someone wanted to buy the ocean, how would you divide it up? Native Americans felt that land was just like the sea and sky—impossible to own. But the European colonists, especially the French and English, thought otherwise. Each country wanted it all. But each needed the help of the Native Americans to win dominion over America. And that led to a fierce fight and a cry of ...

WHOSE SIDE ARE YOU ON?

A battle was brewing between England and France. No way were they going to share America! Where did that leave America's first people—the nations who had called this land home for so many thousands of years? It left them caught in the middle of a big, messy, war!

STAYING ALIVE
★

The Native Americans could see their world falling apart before their eyes. The Europeans' diseases—smallpox, the flu, and measles—had wiped out their *sachems* (tribal leaders) and young warriors. With so many dead, with the new colonists grabbing more and more land, with the growing knowledge that a bow and arrow was no match for a musket, the Native Americans knew things were going to have to change. Weakened groups, with no one to lead them and no one to protect them, were easy pickings for power-hungry rivals. How could they survive?

A PRAYER AND A PINT
★

Maybe it *was* better to make peace with the Europeans. After all, the French and English had better weapons and useful things to trade for, such as metal pots and sharp knives. Missionaries managed to convince many Native Americans that Christianity was better than their ancient beliefs. And with all the illness and death that had hit the Native Americans when the Europeans arrived, it was easy to believe that perhaps they *had* been abandoned by their sacred spirits.

The Europeans chipped away at the tribal ways with another weapon—alcohol. Rum and whiskey had a powerful effect on the Native Americans' bodies. Just as they had no resistance to the Europeans' diseases, neither could they deal with what liquor did to them. Colonists began to make a point of offering a quick drink before trading, and the Native Americans, their minds clouded by the power of drink, often made really poor deals.

The Native American nations in the eastern parts of North America knew things were changing. The French and the English were here to stay. Some groups started to choose sides. To many, the French seemed the friendliest. They seemed less intent on grabbing land, more interested in simply trading. The English, on the other hand, were growing too fast. Settlers were moving inland, sometimes swindling the Native Americans, or taking land by force.

FACE-OFF!

★

As the British colonists moved further into America's heartland—toward the borders of New France—bad feelings were growing between the French and English. In 1752, a group of Ottawa and Ojibwa warriors, led by French officers, swooped down on a British trading post, killing thirteen Native Americans who had sided with the British. And so began the first of many skirmishes that would lead to the infamous French and Indian War—a bloody battle for control over much of North America. Native Americans ended up fighting on both sides. Ancient rivalries erupted and tribal groups ended up facing off against each other—drawn into someone else's fight.

SURPRISING HISTORY

Only Americans call the French and Indian War by that name. The rest of the world knows this war as the Seven Years War.

It was during the French and Indian War that British troops first started calling the colonial soldiers "Americans." The name stuck.

WASHINGTON'S MISTAKE

George Washington may have become the "father of our country," but he made a mess of things during the early days of the French and Indian War.

Trouble started brewing in what is now the city of Pittsburgh. Back then, it was a wild place marked by a French fort called Fort Duquesne. The governor of Virginia decided that the fort was in Virginia territory. He sent twenty-two-year-old Washington, who was a surveyor (a person who marks the land for mapmaking), out to the fort in 1754. Washington told the French they were trespassing. They told him to get lost.

Angry, Washington returned 4 months later with 150 militiamen and surprised a group of French soldiers, killing 10. Naturally, the French wanted revenge.

Fort Necessity was one of George Washington's worst mistakes during the war. He ordered it built on a swampy marsh. The waters rose when it rained and the fort flooded.

Many people say that this was the event that pushed the fighting between the French and British into full-scale warfare. But the truth is, that fight was brewing from the moment the French and British first arrived on America's shores.

FIVE NATIONS—UNITED

★

Many Native Americans were fierce warriors. Long before the first Europeans came to the New World, warfare was their way. But in time one group grew sick of all the killing and death and signed a peace treaty with some of their enemies, forming a league—The League of Five Nations—a union of the Mohawks, Oneidas, Cayugas, Senecas, and the Onondagas. The members of the league became known as the Iroquois. By 1715, a sixth nation, the Tuscaroras, joined. But they still had enemies.

The Hurons were the Iroquois' rivals and had long dominated the fur trade. Together with the powerful Cherokee nation, they chose to side with France. When the Iroquois heard that the Hurons had chosen the French side, they reluctantly threw their support to the English—in spite of the League's vows to stay out of the fighting.

VIVE LA FRANCE?

★

For the next five years the French and British—along with their Native American allies—skirmished, ambushed, and killed, from the Carolinas to what is now Detroit. For several years France was unstoppable, winning victory after victory. England decided the way to win was by outspending the French, and began pouring mountains of money into getting extra soldiers and weapons. Finally, in September of 1759, the French and British found themselves facing off on the Plains of Abraham, just outside Quebec, in Canada. There, one ten-minute long battle would decide the future of America.

When the smoke cleared and fighting stopped, General Wolfe, the British commander, was dead. The Marquis de Montcalm, the French leader, lay mortally wounded. But the British, who had outnumbered and outmaneuvered the French, had crushed France's army. New France had fallen to the British.

If there hadn't been a war between England and France, there might not be a United States. The war left England almost flat broke. The taxes the British began heaping on the Americans after the war made the colonists fighting mad. During the war, many a "Yankee" (George Washington among them), fought along with the British and learned their tricks and tactics. That knowledge would come in very handy in the coming years.

What if your parents made you pay every time you wanted to

watch TV, play Monopoly, or grab a glass of milk?

What if your mom decided that your bratty cousin should move in and share your

bedroom, without even asking if you'd mind? Bet you'd start…

ACTING UP

The French and Indian War was a grand victory for England. But it created a big problem. Britain had spent way too much money to win, so the Prime Minister, George Grenville, came up with a plan. Make the colonists pay! After all, the war *had* been fought on their soil. Grenville cooked up a new law and called it the Revenue Act of 1764. But the colonists renamed it the Sugar Act. It was a very bitter bit of legislation to swallow.

SWEET AND SOUR
★

Grenville's idea was simple. Make the colonists pay a special tax every time they bought sugar. Now, there had been taxes before. In fact there already was a tax on molasses imported from outside the British Isles—not that the colonists actually *paid* it. Most of the time, it was ignored. After all, England was thousands of miles away. Who was going to know? But this time, things would be different. This wasn't going to be a look-the-other-way tax. Grenville meant business. He sent a slew of customs officials to America to make sure the colonists paid up. The Americans hated that idea. What if the British kept heaping on more taxes?

NON-CENTS!
★

As if the Sugar Act wasn't bad enough, the British had more up their sleeves in 1764. They added the Currency Act to the Americans' burdens. Now the colonists couldn't even issue their own money. Things were getting bad.

STAMP IT OUT
★

Back in Britain, Grenville got word that the colonists were mad and determined to boycott sugar. But Britain *still* needed money. In March of 1765, Grenville surprised the colonists with a new act—the Stamp Act. If an item was made of paper, you had to pay to have a special seal placed on it. Newspapers had to be printed on taxed paper, which cost an extra half-penny a sheet. Books, pamphlets, playing cards, legal forms, and school diplomas all were taxed. Grenville tried to explain that the money raised would help pay for the British troops that were on American soil. What could be fairer?

Added to Britain's demands at the same time was another new act—the Quartering Act. The law said that the colonists might now be forced to house and feed British troops in their homes if there weren't enough public barracks.

The Americans were furious! Protests broke out everywhere and some turned violent. Tax collectors were tarred and feathered—captured, stripped to their birthday suits, covered with hot pine tar, doused with feathers, and paraded through the streets!

SONS AND DAUGHTERS OF LIBERTY

As relations with Britain worsened, a secret society of patriots decided to stop complaining and start taking action. In the years to come, they would burn houses. destroy property, and sometimes torture their enemies.

The Sons of Liberty were started in Massachusetts by a loud-mouthed firebrand named Samuel Adams. They grew from a group called the Committees of Correspondence in the early months of 1765 and met in secret in the colonies' bigger towns, often late at night.

At the age of forty-three, Sam Adams had failed at just about everything he had tried. He had studied law, lost a fortune in business, and even failed as a tax collector. But all those failures were forgotten when he turned to politics, because Sam Adams was a spellbinding speaker. He could whip a crowd into a frenzy!

As Britain lashed out at America, the Sons of Liberty were the first to say, "No way! No how!"

Every time a new act was announced, angry crowds gathered— from New England to Virginia—to protest Britain's actions.

WE'RE WARNING YOU...
★

Those violent protests worked. The Stamp Act was cancelled. But even so, Britain was hard at work dreaming up a new way to keep those upstart colonials in their place. The British were beginning to feel that America needed a good, hard spanking! The curtain was about to go up on the next act—the Declaratory Act. No money was involved here, simply a warning that England had the right to make laws for the colonies "in all cases, whatsoever."

NOT ANOTHER TAX!
★

Many colonists were getting fed up with the British and their taxes and laws. Still, one-fifth of the colonists were loyalists— supporters of England and its king. Another two-fifths simply didn't care one way or the other who was in charge. But a third group wanted a voice in Britain's decisions about the colonies.

In Boston in 1765, Sam Adams and his group, the Sons of Liberty, began making a lot of noise. In October of that same year, representatives from nine colonies met in New York at the Stamp Act Congress to try to figure out what to do. They understood that money had to be raised. They had no problem with that. What they *did* have a problem with was having no say in *how* that money was raised. They felt like kids whose parents wouldn't allow them to make a single decision on their own. But the colonists weren't children.

The new Quartering Act, with its threat of British soldiers moving into people's homes, was getting on everyone's nerves. Each colony was now under pressure to build barracks for the British soldiers as well as pay for all the food and supplies needed by the troops stationed within their borders. At first, this seemed like an okay idea. But as time wore on, the people of New York realized they were paying a lot more than any other colony, simply because there were more troops there. In 1766, they complained. Britain's response? They quickly shut down New York's local government!

How could the colonists make the British understand how they felt?

BOYCOTT BRITAIN!
★

In June of 1767, the man responsible for England's treasury, Charles Townshend, came up with yet another tax plan—the Townshend Acts. New taxes were ordered on a few items, including paper, glass, paint, and tea. Townshend didn't make a big deal about enforcing them at first, so the colonists wouldn't get angry—then he pounced like a cat on a mouse.

This time, the colonists had had enough. They vowed not to buy any of the newly taxed items. It wasn't long before the colonists' refusal to buy British products began hurting the British economy. The colonists were getting far too unruly. This had to stop!

On October 1, 1768, British warships docked in Boston's harbor. Two regiments of soldiers marched through the streets with flags flying and drums beating a warning. The soldiers who arrived were a tough and angry lot. And they had a message for the Americans. Behave—or pay the price!

Name-calling, rock-throwing, ice-pelting—those kinds of behaviors can lead to trouble. And, eventually, they did. British troops stood on one side. Colonial militias stood on the other. Both had guns . But who would fire first?

ARMED AND DANGEROUS

The next three years saw the colonists arguing with the British and the British harassing the colonists right back. Some of the protests turned violent. People were getting hurt.

MASSACRE!
★

On an icy night in 1770, the mood in Boston was edgy. Britain had sent more than 2,000 soldiers into the city—1 soldier for every 6 residents. The Bostonians hated the soldiers and taunted them whenever they could—a shove here, a curse there. Nerves were frayed.

That March 5th night, a single sentry stood guard at the Custom House, Britain's tax headquarters. Several rowdy young men started egging that lone sentry on. Finally, he poked one of the boys. They responded by pelting him with snowballs and hunks of ice. More boys and men gathered around that poor, scared sentry, daring him to fight. Finally, his commander, Captain Thomas Prescott, came to his rescue with seven of the biggest soldiers he could find.

"Go ahead and shoot," the crowd yelled. There was shoving and pushing. One of the soldiers was hit with a stick and fell. As he struggled to his feet, his gun went off. Someone screamed and in the confusion the British fired. When the smoke cleared, three Americans lay dead, among them Crispus Attucks, an African American. Two more would later die from their injuries.

The events of that cold night became a rallying point for the colonists. They called the incident the *Boston Massacre*. It had not been the British soldiers' fault. But there was no telling the angry colonists that!

TEA, ANYONE?
★

Tea might seem like a strange thing to cause a riot. But it did. On May 10, 1773, England announced that the East India Company would now have a complete monopoly on tea in America. Their tea would be sold untaxed and would cost less than any other tea. What could be bad about that?

The colonists smelled something fishy. For one thing, only specially chosen merchants would be allowed to sell the tea. Most American tea sellers were about to be put out of business.

On the chill night of December 16, 1773, over 8,000 people gathered at the Old South Church in Boston. They came to hear Sam Adams, that fierce and fiery Son of Liberty, speak. He dared the crowd to take action—to stop the hated cargo from ever being unloaded on American soil. And take action they did.

Later that evening, the colonists, some dressed as Mohawk Indians with burnt cork smeared on their faces, snuck on board three ships and dumped 342 cases of tea into the harbor.

The punishment was swift and harsh. Boston's port was ordered closed until the Bostonians paid for every leaf of tea that had been tossed into the water. By the end of June 1774, King George III had hit them with four new laws, called the Coercive Acts. The colonists simply called them "intolerable."

COUNTDOWN TO WAR
★

In September of 1774, every colony except Georgia sent a delegate to Philadelphia to be a part of the first Continental Congress. The colonists wanted to make the king understand that things could not continue as they were.

SURPRISING HISTORY

The British soldiers who fired on the colonists were all accused of murder. But John Adams, an ardent patriot, cared passionately about always doing the right thing. He defended the British soldiers in court and had the charges dropped, not because he liked the soldiers, but because he believed in the truth.

With every passing day it seemed as if more and more freedom was being taken away from the Americans. By the beginning of 1775, everyone could sense that war was coming. Rumors were flying. Weapons and ammunition were confiscated. And a Son of Liberty named Patrick Henry inspired the colonists with the stirring words: "Give me liberty or give me death."

MIDNIGHT RIDES
★

The British governor in Massachusetts, General Gage, had his orders. Destroy the colonists' weapons.

On the afternoon of April 18, 1775, a stable boy overheard the news that Gage was going to send 700 men to Concord, a town about 14 miles from Boston, to wipe out the colonists' weapons depot. The boy told Paul Revere—a silversmith, false-tooth maker, and member of the Sons of Liberty—the news.

The colonists were prepared. They had a plan. The only thing they didn't know was how the British would attack—by land or by sea. A signal was arranged. High in the tower of the North Church, the deacon would shine one light at sunset if the redcoats were coming by land, two if by sea. That night, two lights glimmered ever so briefly in the church tower and William Dawes, Dr. Samuel Prescott, and Paul Revere rode out to Concord and nearby Lexington to spread the news that the British were coming. If the British wanted a fight, a fight was what they would get.

READY IN A MINUTE
★

Ready to fight in sixty seconds—that's how the minutemen got their name. On the morning after those midnight rides, 70 minutemen drawn from the Massachusetts militia stood on Lexington Green, determined to stop the British. No one knows who fired first, but once one shot was fired, the guns erupted in a blaze of smoke. The battle lasted only a few minutes, but the British outnumbered the Americans seven to one. Eight Americans died.

The British, feeling cocky, marched on to Concord and began a house-by-house search for weapons. But word spread fast about the deaths at Lexington. Militiamen soon began gathering with revenge on their minds. They would get it. About 400 Americans waited for the British along their return route to Boston, hiding in the bushes. When the shooting stopped, 73 English soldiers were dead and 200 were wounded. The finest soldiers in the world had just been beaten by a badly-equipped, ill-trained group of Americans. The American Revolution had begun!

What would it be—liberty or death? From every colony, north and south, they came to Philadelphia one steamy, sultry summer. Their goal? Nothing short of treason. Their fear? That they would end up hanging for their words. Their mission? Freedom!

I DO DECLARE!

Philadelphia was America's most beautiful city. By 1774, it was also its largest. It was here that a group of America's finest citizens came in May of 1775 to do the unthinkable. They risked their fortunes and their lives. It was a scary thing to do, but it seemed as if there was no other choice.

THE MEETING BEGINS
★

Six months earlier, the First Continental Congress had let Britain and King George III know exactly how upset the colonists were with England's endless taxes. The king had turned a deaf ear. Now, after the fighting at Lexington and Concord, with American blood spilled, it was time to take action!

The Second Continental Congress brought together some of the most powerful men in America—men like Ben Franklin, John Adams, and Virginia's Richard Henry Lee. Everyone quickly got to work. Their first decision? To form an army and appoint George Washington as the commander-in-chief. It was not a moment too soon, for more fighting was about to erupt.

"...THE WHITES OF THEIR EYES"
★

On June 12, war came to Boston. Colonial spies discovered that the British were planning to take control of Dorchester Heights and the Charlestown peninsula, two critical locations for defending the city. The Bostonians decided to sneak into Charlestown first and fortify it before the British could put their plans into action.

Late on the 16th of June, the patriots crept through the dark, across the Charles River toward Bunker Hill. Working through the night, they built a dirt-walled fortification at Breed's Hill, just below. The British commander, General Gage, was furious! He ordered an attack and on June 17th, 2,400 British soldiers boldly marched toward 1,000 poorly-equipped Americans.

"Don't fire until you see the whites of their eyes," an American officer whispered and, somehow, the outnumbered Americans held the hill through two massive assaults. Eventually they had to retreat as their casualties mounted, and the bloodied British took Bunker Hill. Still, a painful lesson had been learned. The Americans were going to be a tough and stubborn foe.

PEACE...PLEASE?

After Bunker Hill (and a lot of discussion) the Continental Congress decided to send King George the *Olive Branch Petition*. It was a hope-filled document, one that said "we can work things out if we try." The King refused to even look at it. Instead, he sent back a note that said the Americans were in deep trouble for being so openly rebellious.

The members of the Continental Congress tried again, explaining why they felt they had to fight. They said that they "resolved to die free men rather than live as slaves."

As the months wore on, Britain's relations with America got worse. In November, Congress figured they'd better start a navy to protect the port cities and asked some European countries for help. And all the while, the fighting continued with a battle here, a loss there, and sometimes a taste of victory. But there was no hope of peace.

UNHAPPY NEW YEAR

January of 1776 saw the publication of a book that became an instant best-seller. Called *Common Sense*, it was written by Tom Paine, a man who had moved to America from England only two years earlier. Paine's words were passionate and strongly written. He said, "We have it in our power to begin the world anew. America shall make a stand, not for herself alone, but for the world." The colonists took the message to heart.

Every day, the situation got more tense. Every day, the Continental Congress took stronger actions, all the while praying for help from Britain's enemies. In April, they declared America's harbors off-limits to British ships and declared that privateers (a nice way of saying pirates) should feel free to raid any British ship. In May, the colonists' prayers for aid were answered when France pledged one million dollars to help defeat their longtime enemy.

As summer began, everyone knew the time had come to do something that would *really* get King George's attention. It was time to tell him that America no longer wanted to be a part of the British empire.

WHY ME?

Thomas Jefferson did not want the job the Continental Congress gave him. He thought John Adams should write the Declaration of Independence. But John Adams said, "I'm obnoxious...and unpopular. You are very much otherwise." So Jefferson began writing one of the most important documents ever penned. He truly believed that even the humblest people had greatness within them. That belief helped him bring so much power to the Declaration.

On June 28th, Jefferson presented his work. Congress had mixed feelings. Some delegates from the middle colonies were still afraid to cut their ties to Britain. But a day later, when word got out that New York City was about to be invaded by a fleet of 30 British warships, the tide turned.

LIFE, LIBERTY, HAPPINESS

After days of arguments, the delegates agreed. A new declaration was read on July 2nd and approved by every colony except New York, which voted to abstain. Still, the delegates fussed with the Declaration and decided that a few paragraphs needed cutting. On July 4th, the final Declaration was read and America declared herself free from British rule.

Many Americans celebrated wildly. Yet many others felt their hearts breaking since they were still loyal to Britain and the king. And both groups knew that America was in for some very hard times.

ARE ALL MEN CREATED EQUAL?

There it was, in plain English: "All men are created equal." But what about the Africans? What about the Native Americans?

Those questions almost destroyed the Declaration of Independence. Thomas Jefferson knew in his heart that slavery was wrong, even though he owned slaves. Still, he included a section against the slave trade. Some delegates felt the way he did. But the delegates from Georgia, South Carolina, and North Carolina thought otherwise. They said they would not sign if any of the parts on slavery remained. John Adams, Ben Franklin, and Thomas Jefferson made a decision. Freedom for America must come first. Without that freedom, how would it ever be possible to free the slaves?

What is the coldest you've ever been? Think about it for a moment. Now imagine yourself ten times colder, sleeping outside in the dead of winter. Can you see yourself taking a ten-mile hike with only rags wrapped around your feet, or firing a ten-ton cannon all day long in one-hundred-degree heat? All this was part of ...

A SOLDIER'S LIFE

The soldiers who fought for America's freedom during the Revolution had it tough. They fought in blistering heat. They crossed chest-deep streams in howling blizzards, then kept on marching in freezing, wet uniforms. They frequently ran out of food and some tried to live on tree bark and shoe leather. As one officer put it, "Many a good lad with nothing to cover him from his hips to his toes save his blanket," kept on fighting. How did they do it?

BOYS TO MEN
★

They came from the busy streets of Boston or the pastures of Pennsylvania. Some were barely sixteen. Others were grizzled old men nearer sixty. But America's men (and some women disguised as men) answered the call to fight for freedom.

Before war broke out, every colony had a militia— a kind of once-in-a-while army. But each militia had their own way of doing things. When a militia from Vermont got together with a group from New Jersey, no one knew what the other was doing. Confusion was costing lives. The first challenge George Washington faced as head of the Continental Army was blending all the different militias into one united fighting force. In 1776, after he begged for money from the Continental Congress, a real army was born. Every state had to send a large group of soldiers to help fight the war. Each soldier would be paid the grand sum of $6.67 a month.

WHAT TO WEAR
★

One of the first problems the new soldiers faced was what to wear. No one could decide on a color for the uniforms. The first soldiers were issued brown jackets, but soon a blue coat (trimmed in different colors depending on where the soldier came from) replaced it. Uniforms were expensive and wore out quickly. Something cheaper was needed. One answer came from a group of born-to-be-wild Pennsylvania riflemen. They wore rugged hunting shirts made from deerskin or homespun cloth.

The shirts were cheap to make, cool in the summer, and when pulled on over a couple of shirts, warm in the winter. That shirt became one of the new army's most useful bits of clothing. George Washington found out that the very sight of it struck terror into the hearts of the British who had had some fierce encounters with those wild riflemen in the past.

SURPRISING HISTORY

When American soldiers weren't fighting the British, they sometimes ended up fighting each other. It was hard to maintain discipline in the army camps, so some pretty tough punishments were used.

One brutal punishment had the misbehaving soldier straddle a wooden sawhorse with two heavy muskets tied to each leg. This was painful after a few minutes—awful after an hour!

MUSIC IN THE AIR

★

You may have seen pictures of drummer boys leading Revolutionary soldiers into battle. Those musicians weren't there for the troops' entertainment. There were seven different drumbeats used, each signaling a different action. One drumbeat woke sleeping soldiers at dawn; another signaled that it was time to get ready to march. A special beat was drummed at bedtime and another warned that an enemy was approaching. Soldiers quickly learned what each signal meant if they wanted to survive.

Colonial men in homespun hunting shirts fought side by side with men in fancier uniforms.

YOU EXPECT ME TO EAT THAT?

★

Army food was flat-out awful. And that was on good days when there was actually food to eat! Groups of six soldiers shared provisions and a big heavy cast-iron kettle which they lugged from spot to spot. While on the march, each soldier got a mangy pound of beef and some flour. That was his ration

for the day. The meat was stuck on a stick and cooked over a fire. The flour was turned into firecakes, a much-hated food item. Flour was mixed with water on a cold rock, then pounded until it turned into a paste. The rock was then placed next to the fire. Burned on the outside, raw on the inside, you had to be really hungry to eat a firecake. Soldiers looked forward to longer encampments when the food was more varied and there was time to bake real bread.

TENT, SWEET TENT

★

During those long encampments, especially during the winter months, the men chopped down trees and built log huts. There were 900 built at Valley Forge. Morristown, in New Jersey, had almost 1,200. On short quick marches, soldiers pitched tents that slept six—as long as you were packed like sardines. Sometimes soldiers slept under the stars as they made their way from north to south.

To pass the time between battles, the men played dice and cards. They read tattered newspapers, some many months old, that were passed around like precious treasures. They also prayed for a fast and lasting peace.

A WOMAN'S WAR

You might think of a battlefield as a place for men only. But many women stayed with their men during the American Revolution. Some even brought their children! Mostly the women cooked and mended torn uniforms. But some fought bravely in battle by pretending to be men. Others worked behind the scenes nursing the wounded and dying.

Mary Ludwig Hays was one of the most famous women of Revolutionary days. You may know her as Molly Pitcher. On a June afternoon in 1778, it was so brutally hot that soldiers were passing out. Molly (her nickname) grabbed a battered old pitcher and started running between the battlefield and a nearby stream. Parched men croaked out her name, "Molly! Pitcher!"

Molly was a dynamo. When her husband was hit by enemy fire, she helped carry him to the surgeon's tent, then ran back and started firing her husband's cannon. Through the whole of that blisteringly hot day, she stood her ground. Happily, when the battle ended, she found that her husband was okay.

There were hundreds of Molly Pitchers during the American Revolution and many a life was saved by these brave young women.

If you think a scraped knee hurts, imagine getting a hot lead musket ball through

your thigh. Does an upset stomach lay you low?

Think about having one while you're on a fifty-mile forced march.

It's no wonder that colonial soldiers often shouted...

I NEED A DOCTOR!

Soldiers in the American Revolution lived life on the edge. They were shot at by the British, and exposed to pelting snow and stifling heat. But most of all, they were exposed to one another. In close quarters, germs hopped from new recruits to the seasoned soldiers and back again. America could not win a war if its troops were throwing up and feverish! In 1776, 1,000 American men were killed in the fighting and 1,200 were wounded. But a staggering 10,000 died from disease.

WHAT'S THE PROBLEM?
★

There were no stethoscopes or thermometers during the Revolution. They hadn't been invented yet. In fact, there were hardly any doctors. America only had about 3,500 doctors, and of those only 200 actually had medical degrees.

Doctors usually tried to cure illnesses by flushing out the bad germs. They did that by giving their patients something to make them throw up. Then, they added laxatives to push the germs out in yet another direction. And colonial doctors believed firmly in the healing powers of bleeding—either by nicking a vein and collecting a pint of blood in a bowl, or attaching leeches, bloodsucking worms.

One doctor put his medical philosophy like this:
When patients come to I
I physics, bleeds,
and sweats 'em.
Then if they choose to die
What's that to I—I lets 'em.

It was definitely dangerous to get sick.

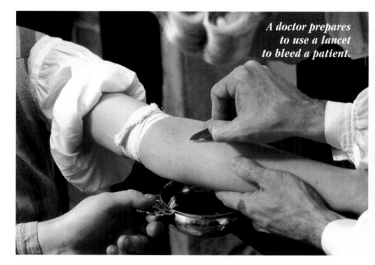
A doctor prepares to use a lancet to bleed a patient.

These fat leeches have just had a blood supper.

FIGHTING THE KILLER POX
★

Just about the deadliest disease to sweep through an army camp was smallpox. Multiply chicken pox by a thousand, and you have an idea what smallpox was like. An outbreak of this nasty illness could thin the ranks faster than a regiment of crack British troops. So, in 1777, George Washington ordered that every soldier in the Continental Army get immunized against this disease.

In those days they didn't have shots like we do today. Instead, they picked off the crusts that had formed on the blisters of men who had developed a mild case of smallpox. Then, with a sharp knife called a lancet, a doctor made a small puncture in the left shoulder of a healthy soldier and worked the dried scab into the skin. A laxative, guaranteed to send the strongest man running to the "necessary" was given, and that was followed by a bloodletting. Finally, the exhausted soldier was allowed to rest in a special tent for a couple of days. But it was worth it. Outbreaks of smallpox became rare events.

BITE THE BULLET

★

Injuries from musket fire and cannon explosions were other major medical emergencies doctors faced. There were no real painkillers and no anesthetics. Injured soldiers were given a bullet to bite on—to keep them from screaming out in pain or biting through their tongues as the doctor tried to help them. Mercifully, most of them fainted when the pain became too great.

There wasn't much doctors could do to help wounded soldiers. For head injuries, they used a tool that looked a bit like a corkscrew to remove a disk of bone from the skull. This released the pressure caused by swelling around the brain.

For serious injuries to arms and legs, doctors usually cut off the limb. After the arm or leg was amputated, hot tar was poured on the stump. This sterilized the wound and stopped the bleeding.

Musket balls that had lodged in the body were pulled out by making an incision with a sharp knife, then reaching in with a special pair of tongs that gripped the ball. The wound was then wrapped in flannel that had been dipped in oil, topped by a dressing of bread and milk. It was almost impossible to keep wounds from getting infected. If a bullet didn't kill a soldier, the infection that followed usually did.

COMING CLEAN

Doctors knew that dirt led to disease. Officers tried to make sure that their troops washed their hands at least once a day and took baths two or three times a week—far more than ordinary citizens.

Three times a week, soldiers paid a visit to the barber for a shave, always at night. Daylight was too precious to be wasted sitting in a barber's chair. Hair was to be neat and combed. Soldiers were supposed to powder their hair once a day. Officers had to have freshly powdered hair for every parade and ceremony.

And answering the call of nature? Army "necessaries" were holes dug at least 300 feet from camp. Every four days (more often in hot weather) they were filled in and new ones dug.

Many women travelled with the soldiers from battle to battle— always there to lend a hand with nursing the sick and wounded.

There was no turning back. War was creeping across the colonies and life

would never be the same again. As word of America's dream of independence spread,

people came forward to serve their new country. Mothers hugged their sons,

and children kissed their fathers good-bye, as they headed...

OFF TO WAR

Farmers left their plows rusting in their fields. Shopkeepers hung "closed" signs on their doors. And from Maine to the Carolinas, Americans set off to fight a war that soon spread to each and every colony.

THE MISFIT ARMY
★

The fighting that began at Lexington and Concord soon crept across New England and up toward Canada. The very first battles proved a rude shock to the Continental Army and its new leader, George Washington.

Washington's army was a mess—over 17,000 men who had never been soldiers before. The new officers didn't know how to issue commands and the enlisted men didn't know how to obey them. One-quarter of the men were too sick to fight.

Still, six months after Bunker Hill, a cocky fighting force of Continental soldiers headed north to Canada to capture Quebec, Britain's last major stronghold in North America. Inexperienced, the troops found themselves marching through blizzards. The frigid weather took its toll, with only 700 of the original 1,100 soldiers who had started the march able to finish. By the time they arrived they were almost too tired to fight! And for a young American general named Benedict Arnold, shot through the leg during the battle, Quebec was the beginning of a strange and twisted career that would take him from hero to villian.

GENTLEMAN GEORGE
★

Determination and dignity pretty much sum up George Washington's character. No matter how often he lost in battle (and he lost a *lot*), no matter how hopeless the war seemed, he quietly stuck with the task at hand. He slept in freezing cold tents, rode through rain and sleet, and constantly risked death. He never looked for greatness. It simply came and found him.

Washington's first test came on August 30, 1776. Unfortunately, he failed. His troops suffered a crushing defeat at the Battle of Long Island, in New York. More than 2,000 Continental soldiers were killed, wounded, or taken prisoner. A few weeks later, Manhattan fell to the British—and was soon in flames as deliberately set fires destroyed over 500 buildings.

Another major battle broke out in White Plains, New York, in late October. British troops, under experienced leaders, simply outsmarted the Americans. Stung by another bitter loss, Washington slunk off across the Hudson River to New Jersey to figure out what he could possibly do to turn defeat into victory.

AMERICA'S FIRST SPY

Nathan Hale was only twenty-one when he volunteered to spy for George Washington. Dressed as a Dutch schoolteacher, he snuck behind the British lines and wrote down what he saw in Latin. Alas, he was captured. As a hangman's noose was tightened around his neck, Hale calmly said, "I only regret that I have but one life to lose for my country"— words that inspired a nation.

A CHRISTMAS SURPRISE
★

Washington decided to go for broke. December 1776 dragged to a cold and bitter end. Fighting the war the British way wasn't working. Washington felt it was time for a different strategy. He chose Christmas Eve to make his move. Quietly, his troops—2,400 men bundled in rags to keep warm—rowed across the Delaware River to Trenton, New Jersey. There, 1,200 mercenary German soldiers, called Hessians, were camped. The Hessians had been hired by the British and they were a dangerous foe. Fortunately for Washington, they were in no shape to fight on Christmas Day, since they had partied too much the night before. Surrender was swift (most of the Hessians were still asleep) and America finally had a much-needed triumph.

THE THRILL OF VICTORY...
★

Washington's good luck stayed with him through the first battle of 1777. The Continental Army won a surprise victory at Princeton, New Jersey. Again, Washington used sly tactics to get himself out of trouble, sneaking away from one position and moving to another under the cover of darkness. He wrapped cannon wheels with rags to muffle their noise, then left a small group of men behind with orders to bang on pots and make a racket. By sunrise, the Americans had snuck up on the unsuspecting British troops from the side. Lord Cornwallis, the British general, was caught completely by surprise!

THE AGONY OF DEFEAT
★

1777 would be a year of ups and downs for the Americans. They lost a battle in Brandywine, Pennsylvania, when Washington misjudged the enemy's position. They lost a battle in Germantown, also in Pennsylvania, when they got caught in a thick fog. But up in New York's Hudson Valley, the news was a bit better.

General John Burgoyne was in charge of the British forces there, and he was waging a winning fight. But he, too, made a mistake when he decided to move his troops from Canada to Albany—a 350-mile journey. It took months and his supplies ran low. Burgoyne cut through Vermont, aiming to raid the town of Bennington for food and supplies. Instead he ran right into a trap set by General John Stark. Stark's ragtag group of American militiamen had melted down pewter spoons and plates to make musket balls, then disguised themselves as Americans still loyal to Britain. Britain lost 900 men in the battle that followed.

Still Burgoyne managed to press on. He was determined to drive a wedge between the Northern and Middle colonies. In Saratoga, New York, on October 17, 1777, he faced off against America's General Horatio Gates. When the smoke settled over the battlefield, 1,400 British soldiers were dead and the other 6,000 simply laid down their arms and quit.

WINTER OF DEATH
★

The winter of 1778 was brutal—cold and damp. Washington moved his army to Valley Forge, a bleak hilltop about 18 miles northwest of Philadelphia. In spite of Gates' victory at Saratoga, it was the lowest point in the war for Washington.

There was no food. It was freezing and many men had no shoes. Some wore tattered rags instead of pants! Over 2,000 soldiers died that winter from sickness. Again and again, Washington begged the Continental Congress for supplies—but none came. But throughout that long winter, whenever the weather warmed enough so that the men could leave their log huts, they worked at becoming better soldiers.

General Washington brought in a German aristocrat who didn't speak a word of English. Baron von Steuben worked tirelessly. He screamed and swore, day in and day out, teaching the new soldiers the proper way to load rifles and fight in formation, as an aide translated his tirades into English. Eventually, motivated by the feisty foreigner, the scraggly American troops started to move and think as a winning team.

Finally, toughened by a winter of sacrifice, the Americans were ready to fight…and win.

War brought muffled drumrolls, the dull pounding of thousands of feet coming closer and closer, explosions of fire and smoke, and the stink of gunpowder in the air. There were cries and moans from the fallen soldiers, and...

BLOOD ON THE BATTLEFIELDS

"These are the times that try men's souls," Tom Paine wrote in an essay called *Crisis*. "The summer soldier and the sunshine patriot will, in this crisis, shrink from the service of their country; but he that stands it *now*, deserves the love and thanks of man and woman." It was easy to be a soldier when things were going well. But America's War for Independence was rough going. For eight miserable long years the cannons blasted, troops marched, and people died.

ROUGH AND READY

The long winter at Valley Forge was a turning point for the Continental Army. They had survived the terrible winter. By late spring, Washington had well-trained troops, ready for a fight. They got that fight on June 28, 1778, and won a big victory at the Battle of Monmouth in New Jersey.

Another American victory was a diplomatic one. France and the Continental Congress signed an official agreement. In August, a fleet of French warships arrived, but got caught in a storm and had to anchor in Boston for repairs. Still, France had thrown their support to the Americans. Money and more soldiers would soon be on the way.

SURPRISING HISTORY

Over 10,000 African Americans earned their freedom from slavery fighting in the Continental Army. But many more chose to fight for Britain.

In the Northern regiments, almost 1 in 5 soldiers was of African descent.

AMERICA'S FIRST "CIVIL WAR"

A different struggle ripped America apart as the war dragged on. Many colonists had stayed loyal to King George and chose to fight on the side of the British. Families were split apart. Brothers fired against their brothers.

Who were these loyalists? Some were African-American slaves, who had been promised their freedom in exchange for fighting for the British. Some were Native Americans, who believed that the British would be less likely to steal away more of their lands. Most were people who distrusted the wild ways of the revolutionaries and felt comfortable with things "the way they were."

The loyalists were hated by the people who wanted independence, and, from time to time, ugly fights broke out between the two groups. Savage raids against the loyalists lead to violence, and death.

Because there were many more loyalists in the Southern colonies, the British decided to move the fighting south. And so the war that had long been fought in New England and the Middle colonies took a turn southward.

ALL-AMERICAN HEROES
★

The British were discovering just how feisty the Americans could be, as colonists with spirit to spare made the Redcoats' lives miserable. There was "Mad" Anthony Wayne, who used bayonets and axes to chop his way into the British-held fort at Stony Point in New York. There was John Paul Jones, an American naval captain, whose brash cry of "I have not yet begun to fight" led to a stunning victory against one of the British Navy's finest ships. As tales of these heroics swept through the Continental Army encampments, they inspired America's battle-weary soldiers to press on.

A SEESAW WAR
★

By 1780, *everyone* was tired of fighting. As the troops swung south, America suffered yet another big loss in Charlestown, South Carolina, on May 12th. The British called it revenge for their stunning defeat at Saratoga, New York. Americans, hopeful for a swift victory to end the war, saw their dreams dashed.

George Washington sent a reluctant Rhode Islander named General Nathanael Greene to take control of the Continental Army in the South. Greene was a very creative soldier, but he was commanding an army that barely had guns and ammunition. It was going to take a lot of creativity to overcome those odds.

Washington had several shocks awaiting him. There was the treachery of Benedict Arnold, a trusted friend (see below). In addition, many of the Continental Army's troops were threatening to mutiny over the lack of food and pay. 1780 was turning out to be a very tough year!

TURNCOAT!

Benedict Arnold could have been one of America's greatest war heroes. He fought boldly in battle and was wounded twice. But he was also bossy and boastful, and many soldiers disliked him. In spite of that, Washington promoted him to commandant of Philadelphia after the British left the city.

There, Arnold fell in love with a pretty 19-year-old named Peggy Shippan who adored giving lavish parties—too many parties! Arnold soon ran out of money, so he got involved in several shady business deals. Congress found out and recommended a court-martial. Faced with financial ruin, Arnold made a desperate decision: For a million dollars he would deliver the plans for West Point, one of America's most important garrisons, to England.

Caught red-handed, he escaped and joined the British side. America's traitor became Britain's hero.

WOULD IT EVER END?
★

South Carolina was still the scene of bloody fighting as another year began. A British commander named Sir Banastre Tarleton broke the traditional rules of war by killing retreating American soldiers after several skirmishes had ended. That made the Americans so mad, they nicknamed him 'the Butcher' and vowed revenge. They got it in the little town of Cowpens, South Carolina, on January 17, 1781.

There, Tarleton met his match in stubborn Daniel Morgan—a frontiersman and all-around spitfire, who tricked the British Butcher by pretending to retreat. Tarleton followed and rode straight into a trap. Four regiments were waiting to encircle the British forces, but the slippery Tarleton managed to escape. Over 830 other British soldiers were not so fortunate.

Victory seesawed to the British side when, three months later, Lord Cornwallis scored a victory at the Battle at Guilford Courthouse in North Carolina. But it was a hollow victory, for his men suffered massive casualties. Britain, and fresh troops, were far away. The British were getting hammered by Spanish troops in Florida and Dutch sailors on the high seas. The Americans knew Cornwallis's supplies were running low. It was time to strike.

VICTORY...OR DEATH!
★

George Washington made the most important decision of the American Revolution. He, and a French general named Rochambeau, sent their armies on a 500-mile journey from Rhode Island to Yorktown, Virginia. Once there, they worked through the night to dig deep trenches. By daybreak, the British found they were trapped—surrounded on all sides. That day, September 30, 1781, marked the beginning of a siege that led to America's final victory. On October 19th, Britain surrendered to America. The war was over at last.

America's long struggle left thousands dead and many more wounded.

America had won its independence, but the long road toward becoming a nation

still lay ahead. In the years that followed, the new citizens

of the United States of America would often ask…

NOW WHAT DO WE DO?

The American Revolution officially came to an end on September 3, 1783, when a treaty was signed in Paris, France. But the end of the war was the beginning of some very hard times. America's colonies, which had bonded so tightly in their fight against the British, found themselves drifting apart. America had won its freedom. We had become the United States of America. But no one could agree on what to do next.

PEACE AT LAST?
★

For the soldiers who had been at war for so many years, coming home would be sweet, yet also very difficult. Farmers who had left their fields to go off and fight came back to bills unpaid, weed-choked land, and families they barely recognized. They were the lucky ones! Many thousands of Americans died in the war. Those who survived carried permanent scars and some would never be able to work again.

America's fight with the British might have ended, but there were still deadly skirmishes with the Native Americans as colonists pushed further inland. A growing rift began to form over the issue of slavery in the new states. There was even a battle brewing about who was going to be in charge of America.

Now that King George was out of the picture, one of George Washington's officers suggested that Washington use his army to take control of the states and proclaim himself king. Another King George for America? Fortunately, Washington said "no."

A BIG MESS
★

Life in the new United States was proving difficult. For starters, each state had its own currency. And during the war, when everyone needed lots of money, many states had printed too many dollar bills. After the war, all that paper became almost worthless, and you sometimes needed a stack of bills as big as a loaf of bread to buy that bread. Some states wouldn't accept another state's money, which made things difficult if you were traveling.

There was still fighting over who owned new territories as the states pushed their boundaries west—endless arguments as everyone bickered over where their borders really ended. Small states were worried that they were going to get pushed around by bigger states. There was even talk of turning the thirteen colonies into three separate countries!

For the loyalists, who had supported Britain during the war, life in the brand-new United States was impossible. Over 100,000 people packed up their belongings and sailed for Canada to make a new life.

For the African-American loyalists, the choices were more complicated. Some also went to Canada, but many more returned to Africa to start a new colony of their very own. It was called Sierra Leone and it was funded by a group of wealthy Englishmen who felt guilty about the evils of slavery.

America's first people—the Native Americans—were forced onto ever-smaller bits of land. Years of struggle and bloodshed still lay ahead.

WHO'S IN CHARGE HERE?
★

The members of the Continental Congress struggled to put a plan together to keep the new states from drifting apart. But because America had just shaken itself loose from one snooty king and his pushy ministers, Congress was terrified of putting *anyone* in charge. For a while they couldn't even agree on what to call the new nation! How were they going to figure out how to run it?

Some of the men who had been a part of the Continental Congress tried to write a set of laws. The first ones they came up with were called the Articles of Confederation, which were approved while the American Revolution was still being fought in July, 1778. The Articles sounded good on paper, but they had no bite. Power still lay with each state.

A government needs money. Congress had no way to get any other than to ask each state to contribute funds. Big states and small states had the same vote in everything. Not only was this system unfair, it wasn't working. Soon the new government was flat broke. In a humiliating turn of events, Congress was chased out of Philadelphia in 1781 by angry soldiers who had never gotten paid money owed them for fighting in the Revolution.

SURPRISING HISTORY

George Washington was the first President of the United States, right? Wrong! Actually, John Hanson was appointed the first official President of the United States in 1781. He was appointed under the Articles of Confederation. His job was to run the meetings of the Continental Congress, and little more. Six other presidents followed him, each serving for one year, before Washington took office under a new set of rules—the United States Constitution!

One of the jobs for the leaders of Congress, was to come up with a motto for the new nation. They chose *E Pluribus Unum*—Latin for "from many, one."

WANTED: NEW HEROES
★

On December 13, 1783, George Washington stood before the Continental Congress and said good-bye to all his friends, and to his life as a soldier. For the last nine years, he had slept in dozens of different beds and eaten in hundreds of different places. He wanted to go home to his farm and his wife—to sleep late and feel the warm air of a Virginia morning in spring.

But America still needed all the heroes it could find if it was going to survive. The fragile union of thirteen states was crumbling. During the next four long years, the new nation struggled to find its way. In some places, there was even talk of asking Britain to take the colonies back.

In 1787, Washington returned to the chambers of the Continental Congress, ready to do whatever his country asked. He was joined by an old and ailing Ben Franklin, and John Adams. New heroes came, too—Alexander Hamilton and James Madison among them. They were all determined to hammer out a new government, no matter how long it took.

"Freedom is a light for which many men have died in darkness." Those words are carved into a tomb for an unknown soldier from the American Revolution. Things might have looked gloomy for the new United States in its earliest days, but we were definitely on our way.

More than two hundred years later, their words still bring their world to life. These are the actual thoughts and feelings of people just like you, who faced some difficult times and longed for a better world.

IN THEIR OWN WORDS

"OH SHAME UPON YOU, COWARDS!"

★

As they suffered defeat after defeat, many Americans began to doubt whether they could ever really win. A group of men were arguing one night that it might be better if they just gave up. After all, the British had offered a pardon to anyone who surrendered. One of the men's wives, Hannah White Arnett, happened to overhear their argument and started yelling at them. Her tirade did the trick. Every man in the room remained loyal to the American cause.

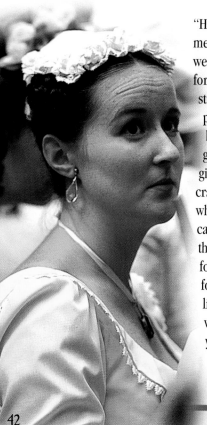

"Have you chosen the part of men or traitors? We are poor, weak, and few, but God is fighting for us. We entered into this struggle with pure hearts and prayerful lips. And now, *now* because for a time the day is going against us, you would give up all and sneak back like cravens to kiss the feet of those who trampled upon us? And you call yourselves men! The sons of those who gave up home and fortune and fatherland to make for themselves and for dear liberty a resting place in the wilderness! Oh shame upon you, cowards!"

"WE ARE TIRED OUT IN MAKING COMPLAINTS"

★

Thayendanegea, which means "he who places two bets," lived in two very different worlds. He was a Mohawk chief, but he was also known by the English as Joseph Brant. He was sent to a charity school as a boy and became an interpreter for a British missionary. At the age of thirteen, he fought in the French and Indian War and kept close ties with the British. When the American Revolution broke out he faced a difficult problem. He sided with the British—a decision that split the Iroquois League in half. He felt that the colonists would simply take everything away from his people if America won the war.

"The Mohawks have on all occasions shown their zeal and loyalty to the Great King; yet they have been very badly treated by his people. Indeed it is very hard, when we have let the King's subjects have so much of our land for so little value. We are tired out in making complaints and getting no redress....Every man of us thought that, by fighting for the King, we should ensure for ourselves and our children a good inheritance."

"IN THESE WRETCHED HOVELS WERE WE PENNED AT NIGHT"

★

By the time America went to war with Britain, one in six colonists were African Americans. Ninety-nine percent of them were slaves, living under the most horrid conditions. Josiah Henson described his dreadful life on a slave plantation.

"We lodged in log huts, and on the bare ground. Wooden floors were an unknown luxury. In a single room were huddled, like cattle, ten or a dozen persons, men, women, and children. All ideas of refinement and decency were, of course, out of the question. Our beds were collections of straw and old rags, thrown down in the corners and boxed in with boards; a single blanket the only covering. The wind whistled and the rain and snow blew in through the cracks, and the damp earth soaked in the moisture till the floor was muddy as a pig-sty. Such were our houses. In these wretched hovels were we penned at night, and fed by day; here were the children born and the sick neglected."

"I SAW SEVERAL OF THE MEN ROAST THEIR OLD SHOES AND EAT THEM"

★

Joseph Plumb Martin was only fifteen when he enlisted in the Continental Army. The pride and confidence he felt when he joined up soon gave way to boredom and, during the brutal days at Valley Forge, a lot of suffering. This is his description of that bleak time.

"We were absolutely literally starved. I do solemnly declare that I did not put a morsel of victuals into my mouth for four days and as many nights, except a little black birch bark which I gnawed off a stick of wood, if that can be called victuals. I saw several of the men roast their old shoes and eat them, and I was afterwards informed…that some of the officers killed and ate a favorite little dog that belonged to one of them. If this is not 'suffering' I request to be informed what can pass under the name."

SURPRISING HISTORY

If they knew how to write, most people kept journals in the 1700s. Some were rich and famous like Ben Franklin. But many others were barely educated folk who recorded the smallest details of everyday life. Even soldiers of the Revolution, out on long marches, recorded their thoughts on bits and scraps of paper. How amazing it is that any of these scraps survived!

Who says you can't travel through time? Eat dinner in a tavern with no electricity. Watch a wall of British soldiers marching straight toward you, guns at the ready. Try your hand at cleaning and spinning freshly shorn sheep's wool. And remember to cover your ears when the cannons blast. You're about to take…

A STEP BACK IN TIME

WILLIAMSBURG AND CARTER'S GROVE, VIRGINIA
★

America's most wonderful living history museum brings you back into the thick of the action just months before the colonies told King George exactly what they thought of him! You'll find plenty to see and do here, from authentic candlelit taverns to horse-drawn carriages. There are shops selling lovely colonial wares such as mob caps and birch root, a courthouse where you can attend a trial, and a jail—grim and dark with chains still hanging from the walls. You can chat with a reenactor playing Patrick Henry, or argue with Lord Dunmore, the British governor. Perhaps you'll want to drill with the militia, or pray for peace in a 300-year-old church.

The Williamsburg complex includes Carter's Grove, once home to over 1,000 slaves. Here you'll get a glimpse of a slave's life. There are special events like weddings, where you'll learn what "jumping the broom" means, and you'll see how African Americans triumphed over their harsh lives.

HISTORIC HUDSON VALLEY, NEW YORK
★

Just 35 miles from New York City, but three hundred years in the past, are two enchanting sites. Phillipsburg Manor re-creates an early 1700s farm, complete with a working mill. Among the special events during the year are the "Legend of Sleepy Hollow" weekend, which includes a visit from the Headless Horseman himself.

Ten miles up the road is Van Cortlandt Manor—a Dutch manor house from the late 1700s. There are hands-on activities, from weaving to cooking, and lavish costume balls take place several times a year.

BOSTON & LEXINGTON, MASSACHUSETTS

★

Begin in Boston and follow the red stripe that marks the Freedom Trail. You can walk through Paul Revere's bedroom, sit in a church pew in the Old North Church, or toss tea into the harbor at the Boston Tea Party Museum. And depending on what time of year you are there, you can see some of the major events that led to the Revolution being reenacted before your very eyes—such as the snowball fight that turned into the Boston Massacre, held every year in December.

In nearby Lexington, celebrate the anniversary of the battle that began the American Revolution as British troops and minutemen face off on the village green.

PHILADELPHIA & VALLEY FORGE, PENNSYLVANIA

★

Start your visit at Independence Hall in Philadelphia. Eat lunch off pewter plates at the same tavern John Adams did. And walk along the same cobbled streets where Tom Jefferson argued with Ben Franklin. Various costumed reenactors appear throughout the year.

Then make the 18-mile drive to Valley Forge and walk the fields where America's soldiers suffered so. Lie in a typical soldier's bunk in a rough-hewn cabin. And visit George Washington's headquarters, where you can run your hands along the very same banister he used.

AMERICA'S PAST...LIVE!

You can see most major events of the war come to life.

Almost all the major battle sites hold reenactments close to or on the date the battles actually occurred. From Vermont and New Hampshire to New Jersey and the Carolinas, there are chances to see the events as they happened. Call the local chambers of commerce for more information.

YORKTOWN, VIRGINIA

★

Celebrate the war's end with a visit to the place where it happened. Hear the cannons roar. Pull on a soldier's coat and hat and sleep in a rough canvas tent. Talk to the camp doctor and experience camp discipline. And savor the peace that hangs over this last great battleground of America's War for Independence.

45

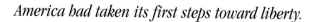

America had taken its first steps toward liberty. It had begun the difficult task of creating a government for the people and by the people. The coming years would bring even more change. Our nation would start to grow stronger and stronger. But it would also face new challenges.

LOOKING FOR FREEDOM

Could there ever be liberty for all? In the coming years, an important new set of laws would be written—the Constitution of the United States of America. Those laws began with the words, "We the people of the United States." But for Native Americans and the African-American slaves, "we the people" did not apply.

Native Americans would see more of their land taken from them, their finest warriors killed, and their nations destroyed. African Americans, living hopelessly with the horror of slavery, would cry out for freedom. Old enemies from across the sea, looking for a fight, would strain the resources of the infant United States. But just as a baby learns to walk by falling down and getting up, over and over again, so too, did America slowly learn to right its many wrongs. Our new nation fell down plenty of times in the years that followed the American Revolution. But somehow, we managed to dust ourselves off and walk proudly into a new century!

WITH GRATEFUL THANKS
This book would not have been possible without the help and cooperation of these wonderful people and organizations. They are:

Cathy Grosfils at The Colonial Williamsburg Foundation

Burns Patterson at Historic Hudson Valley

Douglas Southard at the Bostonian Society

The staff at the Boston Tea Party Museum

Very special thanks to my children, Alex and Tish Scolnik and my husband, Lou, who spent months reliving history. Thanks also to Ms. Elizabeth Yohan's 5th grade history classes at the Increase Miller School.

READ MORE ABOUT IT
★

It is impossible to fit one hundred years into the pages of one book. Here are some titles that offer other glimpses of this fascinating century:

Dear America: The Winter of Red Snow: The Revolutionary War Diary of Abigail Jane Stewart, Valley Forge, Pennsylvania, 1777 by Kristiana Gregory; Scholastic, 1997

A Young Patriot: The American Revolution as Experienced by One Boy by Jim Murphy; Scholastic, 1997

The Revolutionary Soldier: 1775–1783 by C. Keith Wilbur; The Globe Pequot Press, 1997

A History of US: Making Thirteen Colonies by Joy Hakim; Oxford University Press, 1993

The Historic Community Series by Bobbie Kalman; Crabtree Publishing Company

GO ONLINE TO THE PAST
★

There are dozens of wonderful Web sites that focus on American history. These are but a few:

Visit Colonial Williamsburg without leaving home. You'll find games, stories, activities, and virtual visits to the entire area:
http://www.history.org

This link provides excellent timelines of the major events of the American Revolution:
http://www.historyplace.com/index.html

African-American history is at your fingertips. This site will take you to several different Web locations that focus on slavery and on the experiences of free Blacks in colonial times:
http://www.seacoastnh.com/blackhistory/hotlinks.html

Native American history can be found at many locations on the Web. This will lead you to some of the best sites:
http://www.ilt.columbia.edu/k12/naha/nanav.html

PHOTO CREDITS
★

INDEX